Editorial Project Manager
Lorin E. Klistoff, M.A.

Illustrator
Alexandra Artigas

Cover Artist
Barb Lorseyedi

Managing Editor
Ina Massler Levin, M.A.

Creative Director
Karen J. Goldfluss, M.S. Ed.

Art Production Manager
Kevin Barnes

Art Coordinator
Renée Christine Yates

Imaging
James Edward Grace

Publisher
Mary D. Smith, M.S. Ed.

Full-Color STANDAR...

LANGUAGE ARTS
Activities & Games

Includes Standards & Benchmarks

START (subject) START (predicate) START (subject) START (predicate)

Many students read the new book.

Authors

Judy Kvaale, M.S., Sue Lundgren, M.S., and Jennifer Von Pinnon, M.S.

The classroom teacher may reproduce copies of materials in this book for classroom use only. Reproduction of any part for an entire school or school system is strictly prohibited. No part of this publication may be transmitted, stored, or recorded in any form without written permission from the publisher.

Teacher Created Resources, Inc.
6421 Industry Way
Westminster, CA 92683
www.teachercreated.com
ISBN: 978-1-4206-8717-0
©2007 Teacher Created Resources, Inc.
Made in U.S.A.

Teacher Created Resources

Table of Contents

*All standards listed above are from *A Compendium of Standards and Benchmarks for K–12 Education* (Copyright 2004 McREL, www.mcrel.org/standards-benchmarks) Language Arts (Grades 3–5).

Introduction

You just finished teaching a fantastic lesson on guide words, and now you need to know, "Do my students get it?" You do not want to give out a worksheet because your students are tired of sitting. Why not try a game to assess the skill?

There is a great need to replace the traditional paper and pencil means of reinforcing language arts skills with engaging games and activities. *Standards-Based Language Arts Activities & Games* (Grades 3 and 4) is a collection of games that reinforce your language instruction while enabling you to quickly assess your students. Because many of the games are modeled after familiar games, your instructional time is decreased while learning time is increased. The "teacher-friendly" games are designed to connect with any language arts curriculum while addressing the McREL language arts standards and benchmarks.

Each language arts game includes the following components to assist teachers with planning and implementation.

- **Skill:** The language arts skill is addressed in each game.

- **Standards and Benchmarks:** The standards and benchmarks are taken from *A Compendium of Standards and Benchmarks for K-12 Education* (Copyright 2004 McREL, www.mcrel.org/standards-benchmarks) Language Arts (Grades 3–5).

- **Materials:** The list of materials needed to play the games successfully.

- **Suggested Use:** This area lists the possible ways the game can be implemented.

  Cooperative Groups (Small, independent learning groups of two to four students facilitated by a teacher, teacher's aide, parent, etc.)

  Home Connection (A school-to-home link enabling parents to become involved in their child's learning by reinforcing skills taught at school.)

  Teacher Led (The teacher leads the students in a whole-group game or activity.)

  Tutorial (This is one-on-one instruction with a teacher or teacher's aide providing the student with additional practice of the skill.)

  Centers (The student independently plays the game reinforcing the previously taught skill.)

- **Directions:** This lists detailed and easy-to-follow instructions on how to play the game and how it is to be used by teachers, parents, volunteers, etc.

- **Variations:** This area lists additional ideas on how to use the game.

- **Reminder:** This area lists quick and helpful definitions of the targeted skill with examples.

Crazy A

Skill: adjectives

Standard: uses grammatical and mechanical conventions in written compositions

Benchmark: uses adjectives in written compositions (e.g., indefinite, numerical, predicate adjectives)

Materials

- Crazy A cards

Suggested Use

- cooperative groups
- centers
- home connection
- tutorial

Directions (2–4 players)

1. Five cards are dealt to each player and the remaining cards are placed face down as a draw pile. The top card is turned over and becomes the starter card in the discard pile.
2. Player A begins by placing a card from his or her hand that matches the same adjective category (color, number, taste or size) as on the starter card on the discard pile. For example, if a color adjective is shown, another color adjective must be played on top of it.
3. A Wild Card may be played to change the play to any category. A Crazy A card may be played to change the play to the category shown on the Crazy A card.
4. If players do not have a match, they must draw a card from the draw pile. The player may discard if it is a match. If a card cannot be played, it is the next player's turn.
5. When the last card in the pile is drawn, the top card from the discard pile is kept face up while the other cards are shuffled and become the new draw pile.
6. Play continues until one player has discarded all his or her cards.

Variation

- Teachers may choose to use all or some of the categories.

Reminder

An <u>adjective</u> is a word that describes a noun.
Examples: red, hot, several

few

many

one

hundred

fifteen

sixty

some

several

Teacher Created Resources

Teacher Created Resources

Teacher Created Resources

Teacher Created Resources

Teacher Created Resources

Teacher Created Resources

Teacher Created Resources

Teacher Created Resources

Teacher Created Resources

Teacher Created Resources

Teacher Created Resources

Teacher Created Resources

Teacher Created Resources

Teacher Created Resources

Teacher Created Resources

Teacher Created Resources

Teacher Created Resources

Teacher Created Resources

Teacher Created Resources

Teacher Created Resources

Teacher Created Resources

Teacher Created Resources

Teacher Created Resources

Teacher Created Resources

Teacher Created Resources

Teacher Created Resources

Teacher Created Resources

Teacher Created Resources

Teacher Created Resources

Teacher Created Resources

Teacher Created Resources

Teacher Created Resources

Teacher Created Resources

Teacher Created Resources

enormous

large

huge

small

tiny

skinny

tall

short

gigantic

Teacher Created Resources

Teacher Created Resources

Teacher Created Resources

Teacher Created Resources

Teacher Created Resources

Teacher Created Resources

Teacher Created Resources

Teacher Created Resources

Teacher Created Resources

Teacher Created Resources

Teacher Created Resources

Teacher Created Resources

Teacher Created Resources

Teacher Created Resources

Teacher Created Resources

Teacher Created Resources

Teacher Created Resources

Teacher Created Resources

Teacher Created Resources

Teacher Created Resources

Teacher Created Resources

Teacher Created Resources

Teacher Created Resources

Teacher Created Resources

Teacher Created Resources

Teacher Created Resources

Teacher Created Resources

Teacher Created Resources

Teacher Created Resources

Teacher Created Resources

Teacher Created Resources

Teacher Created Resources

Teacher Created Resources

Teacher Created Resources

Teacher Created Resources

Teacher Created Resources

sour

sweet

bitter

spicy

salty

tangy

fruity

tart

bland

©Teacher Created Resources, Inc.

pink

red

white

purple

brown

orange

yellow

green

blue

Teacher Created Resources

Teacher Created Resources

Teacher Created Resources

Teacher Created Resources

Teacher Created Resources

Teacher Created Resources

Teacher Created Resources

Teacher Created Resources

Teacher Created Resources

Teacher Created Resources

Teacher Created Resources

Teacher Created Resources

Teacher Created Resources

Teacher Created Resources

Teacher Created Resources

Teacher Created Resources

Teacher Created Resources

Teacher Created Resources

Teacher Created Resources

Teacher Created Resources

Teacher Created Resources

Teacher Created Resources

Teacher Created Resources

Teacher Created Resources

Teacher Created Resources

Teacher Created Resources

Teacher Created Resources

Teacher Created Resources

Teacher Created Resources

Teacher Created Resources

Teacher Created Resources

Teacher Created Resources

Teacher Created Resources

Teacher Created Resources

Teacher Created Resources

Teacher Created Resources

Teacher Created Resources

Teacher Created Resources

Teacher Created Resources

Teacher Created Resources

Teacher Created Resources

Teacher Created Resources

Teacher Created Resources

Teacher Created Resources

Teacher Created Resources

Teacher Created Resources

Teacher Created Resources

Teacher Created Resources

Teacher Created Resources

Teacher Created Resources

Teacher Created Resources

Teacher Created Resources

Teacher Created Resources

Teacher Created Resources

Teacher Created Resources

Teacher Created Resources

Teacher Created Resources

Teacher Created Resources

Teacher Created Resources

Teacher Created Resources

Teacher Created Resources

Teacher Created Resources

Teacher Created Resources

Teacher Created Resources

Teacher Created Resources

Teacher Created Resources

Teacher Created Resources

Teacher Created Resources

Teacher Created Resources

Teacher Created Resources

Antonym Match

Skill: antonyms

Standard: uses the general skills and strategies of the reading process

Benchmark: understands level-appropriate reading vocabulary (e.g., antonyms)

Materials

- Antonym Match game board
- copy game markers on page 16
  (or use paper squares, chips, sticky notes)
- Antonym Match answer key

Suggested Use

- cooperative groups
- centers
- home connection
- tutorial

Directions (2 players)

1. Place the Antonym Match game board between players.

2. Cover all antonyms on the Antonym Match game board with game markers.

3. Player A uncovers two spaces and states if it is an antonym match (for example: *new* and *ancient* would be a match).

4. Player B checks the answer key.

5. If an antonym match is revealed, the player takes the two markers and takes another turn. If a match is not revealed, it is the other player's turn.

6. Play continues until all game markers are removed.

Reminder

An <u>antonym</u> is a word that means the opposite of another word.
Examples: hot/cold, up/down

Antonym Match: Answer Key

new—ancient

strong—weak

float—sink

future—past

open—shut

melt—freeze

late—early

smile—frown

Antonym Match: Game Markers

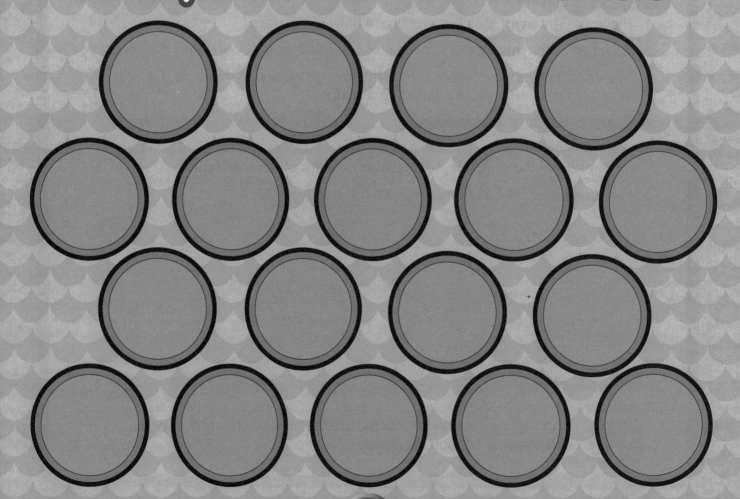

Antonym Match

late	float	strong	ancient
new	future	frown	open
early	freeze	sink	smile
weak	past	shut	melt

Teacher Created Resources

Teacher Created Resources

Teacher Created Resources

Teacher Created Resources

Teacher Created Resources

Teacher Created Resources

Teacher Created Resources

Teacher Created Resources

Teacher Created Resources

Teacher Created Resources

Teacher Created Resources

Teacher Created Resources

Teacher Created Resources

Teacher Created Resources

Teacher Created Resources

Teacher Created Resources

Teacher Created Resources

Teacher Created Resources

Teacher Created Resources

Teacher Created Resources

Teacher Created Resources

Teacher Created Resources

Teacher Created Resources

Teacher Created Resources

Teacher Created Resources

Teacher Created Resources

Teacher Created Resources

Teacher Created Resources

Teacher Created Resources

Teacher Created Resources

Teacher Created Resources

Teacher Created Resources

Teacher Created Resources

Teacher Created Resources

Teacher Created Resources

Star Search

Skill: "be" verbs

Standard: uses grammatical and mechanical conventions in written compositions

Benchmark: uses verbs in written compositions

Materials

- Star Search sentence cards
- Star Search verb cards
- Star Search answer key

Suggested Use

- cooperative groups
- centers
- teacher led
- home connection
- tutorial

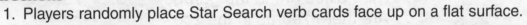

Directions (2 to 4 players)

1. Players randomly place Star Search verb cards face up on a flat surface.

2. Place all Star Search sentence cards face down in a draw pile between players.

3. Player A draws a Star Search sentence card from the pile and finds the Star Search verb card that completes the sentence. He or she keeps the two cards that match. If a player does not have a Star Search verb card to complete the sentence card, the player loses his or her turn.

4. Play continues until all verb cards are removed.

5. Have students check matches against the answer key. The player with the most matches wins.

Reminder

The "be" verb has many different forms such as *am, is, are, was,* and *were.*

Examples: I <u>am</u> a good friend. The parrots <u>are</u> noisy today.

Star Search: Answer Key

am

I <u>am</u> their daughter.
I <u>am</u> a good football player.
<u>Am</u> I the winner today?
I <u>am</u> a clown in the play.
I <u>am</u> the oldest child.
I <u>am</u> the first student in line.
I <u>am</u> a good friend.
<u>Am</u> I the team captain?
I <u>am</u> his student.

are

<u>Are</u> the boats near the dock?
The parrots <u>are</u> noisy today.
Their bikes <u>are</u> in the garage.
<u>Are</u> there zebras in the zoo?
The crayons <u>are</u> in the box.
My friends <u>are</u> at the park.
The five candles <u>are</u> on the cake.
We <u>are</u> going to visit the museum.
<u>Are</u> the dogs in the house?

is

The librarian <u>is</u> busy.
She <u>is</u> sick today.
The cat <u>is</u> not alone.
Our tree <u>is</u> in the front yard.
<u>Is</u> that your pink elephant?
My chair <u>is</u> soft and cozy.
The red wagon <u>is</u> in the sun.
He <u>is</u> not in the race.
<u>Is</u> the dog in the house?

I
_____
their
daughter.

I
_____
a good
football
player.

I the
winner
today?

I
_____ a
clown in
the play.

I
_____ the
oldest
child.

I
_____
the first
student in
line.

I
_____
a good
friend.

I the
team
captain?

I
_____
his
student.

Teacher Created Resources

Teacher Created Resources

Teacher Created Resources

Teacher Created Resources

Teacher Created Resources

Teacher Created Resources

Teacher Created Resources

Teacher Created Resources

Teacher Created Resources

Teacher Created Resources

Teacher Created Resources

Teacher Created Resources

Teacher Created Resources

Teacher Created Resources

Teacher Created Resources

Teacher Created Resources

Teacher Created Resources

Teacher Created Resources

Teacher Created Resources

Teacher Created Resources

Teacher Created Resources

Teacher Created Resources

Teacher Created Resources

Teacher Created Resources

Teacher Created Resources

Teacher Created Resources

Teacher Created Resources

Teacher Created Resources

Teacher Created Resources

Teacher Created Resources

Teacher Created Resources

Teacher Created Resources

Teacher Created Resources

Teacher Created Resources

Teacher Created Resources

_____ the boats near the dock?

The parrots _____ noisy today.

Their bikes _____ in the garage.

_____ there zebras in the zoo?

The crayons _____ in the box.

My friends _____ at the park.

The five candles _____ on the cake.

We _____ going to visit the museum.

_____ the dogs in the house?

Teacher Created Resources

Teacher Created Resources

Teacher Created Resources

Teacher Created Resources

Teacher Created Resources

Teacher Created Resources

Teacher Created Resources

Teacher Created Resources

Teacher Created Resources

Teacher Created Resources

Teacher Created Resources

Teacher Created Resources

Teacher Created Resources

Teacher Created Resources

Teacher Created Resources

Teacher Created Resources

Teacher Created Resources

Teacher Created Resources

Teacher Created Resources

Teacher Created Resources

Teacher Created Resources

Teacher Created Resources

Teacher Created Resources

Teacher Created Resources

Teacher Created Resources

Teacher Created Resources

Teacher Created Resources

Teacher Created Resources

Teacher Created Resources

Teacher Created Resources

Teacher Created Resources

Teacher Created Resources

Teacher Created Resources

Teacher Created Resources

Teacher Created Resources

Teacher Created Resources

26 ©Teacher Created Resources, Inc.

The librarian ___ busy.

She ___ sick today.

The cat ___ not alone.

Our tree ___ in the front yard.

___ that your pink elephant?

My chair ___ soft and cozy.

The red wagon ___ in the sun.

He ___ not in the race.

___ the dog in the house?

Teacher Created Resources

Teacher Created Resources

Teacher Created Resources

Teacher Created Resources

Teacher Created Resources

Teacher Created Resources

Teacher Created Resources

Teacher Created Resources

Teacher Created Resources

Teacher Created Resources

Teacher Created Resources

Teacher Created Resources

Teacher Created Resources

Teacher Created Resources

Teacher Created Resources

Teacher Created Resources

Teacher Created Resources

Teacher Created Resources

Teacher Created Resources

Teacher Created Resources

Teacher Created Resources

Teacher Created Resources

Teacher Created Resources

Teacher Created Resources

Teacher Created Resources

Teacher Created Resources

Teacher Created Resources

Teacher Created Resources

Teacher Created Resources

Teacher Created Resources

Teacher Created Resources

Teacher Created Resources

Teacher Created Resources

Teacher Created Resources

Teacher Created Resources

Teacher Created Resources

Go Figure!

Skill: figurative language
Standard: uses reading skills and strategies to understand and interpret a variety of literary texts
Benchmark: understands the ways in which language is used in literary texts

Materials

- Go Figure! game board
- Go Figure! cards
- Go Figure! answer key
- two colors of game markers (4 per color)

Suggested Use

- cooperative groups
- centers
- home connection
- tutorial

Directions (2 players)

1. Each player chooses a side of the Go Figure! game board and places four game markers on their spots, each player having his or her own game marker color.
2. A player draws a Go Figure! card, reads the sentence and states if it is a metaphor, simile, alliteration, or idiom.
3. If correct, the player moves the game marker diagonally to a connecting spot on the game board that matches the card. For example, if the card is a metaphor, the game marker is moved diagonally to a connecting metaphor spot.
4. If an incorrect answer is given or the connecting spot does not match the card, the player loses the turn.
5. If a diagonal spot is a Free Spot, the player may move a game marker to that spot after correctly stating metaphor, simile, alliteration, or idiom.
6. If a player cannot move, the turn goes to the other player.
7. If a player lands on the Power Spot, that player can jump the opponent's connecting game marker, and the opponent must move the jumped game marker to his or her starting spot.
8. Players continue taking turns until one player's game markers are all on the opposite side of the game board.

Variation

- Players can jump the opponent's game markers.

Reminder

Types of Figurative Language

Alliteration is repeated sounds at the beginning of words.
Example: The pudgy panda played with the purple pail.
Idiom is a phrase or expression with the meaning differing from the literal.
Example: It was raining cats and dogs yesterday.
Metaphor compares two unlike things not using *like* or *as*.
Example: The classroom was a zoo after the program.
Simile compares two unlike things using the words *like* or *as*.
Example: The cloud was like a cotton ball in the sky.

Go Figure!: Answer Key

Alliteration
The green grass grew gradually.
I brought the big black book to Boston.
Chunky chickens chased cheerful chimpanzees.
Many mischievous monkeys made mud pies.
The red raccoon went running down the rocky road.
The lovely lion listened closely to lazy leopards.
The colorful cat crawled into the cold cave.
The big basketball bounced into the battered basket.
The angry alligator ate eight antsy ants.

Idioms
We're all in the same boat.
Time flies when you are busy.
The math assignment was a piece of cake.
It's raining cats and dogs out there today!
Dakota had butterflies in her stomach when she sang a solo.
Maggie was under the weather so she stayed home.
Button your lip!
Does the cat have your tongue?
I have a frog in my throat!

Metaphors
Jordy was a bolt of lightning on the track field.
My sister's room is a pigpen.
The gigantic football player was a bulldozer in the game.
Jill's stomach is a bottomless pit!
His mind is a calculator when working on math problems.
Jenny's new bike turned out to be a lemon.
The clouds were gray blankets hanging in the sky.
The shining stars were sparkling diamonds in the night.
The umbrella was a roof over my head.

Similes
My hands were as cold as ice when I played outside.
The vanilla pudding is as smooth as silk.
The clouds look like cotton balls in the sky.
The joke was so funny that Adam laughed like a hyena!
Santa's belly is as round as a bowl full of jelly.
My younger brother is as stubborn as a mule.
The lake in the morning looks like a sheet of glass.
The excited girl hopped around like a rabbit.
Ava ran to the store as quick as a wink to get some milk.

The green grass grew gradually.

I brought the big black book to Boston.

Chunky chickens chased cheerful chimpanzees.

The lovely lion listened closely to lazy leopards.

The red raccoon went running down the rocky road.

Many mischievous monkeys made mud pies.

The colorful cat crawled into the cold cave.

The big basketball bounced into the battered basket.

The angry alligator ate the eight antsy ants.

Teacher Created Resources

Teacher Created Resources

Teacher Created Resources

Teacher Created Resources

Teacher Created Resources

Teacher Created Resources

Teacher Created Resources

Teacher Created Resources

Teacher Created Resources

Teacher Created Resources

Teacher Created Resources

Teacher Created Resources

Teacher Created Resources

Teacher Created Resources

Teacher Created Resources

Teacher Created Resources

Teacher Created Resources

Teacher Created Resources

Teacher Created Resources

Teacher Created Resources

Teacher Created Resources

Teacher Created Resources

Teacher Created Resources

Teacher Created Resources

Teacher Created Resources

Teacher Created Resources

Teacher Created Resources

Teacher Created Resources

Teacher Created Resources

Teacher Created Resources

Teacher Created Resources

Teacher Created Resources

Teacher Created Resources

Teacher Created Resources

Teacher Created Resources

Teacher Created Resources

Jordy was a bolt of lightning on the track field.

My sister's room is a pigpen.

The gigantic football player was a bulldozer in the game.

Jill's stomach is a bottomless pit!

His mind is a calculator when working on math problems.

Jenny's new bike turned out to be a lemon.

The clouds were gray blankets hanging in the sky.

The umbrella was a roof over my head.

The shining stars were sparkling diamonds in the night.

34

©Teacher Created Resources, Inc.

My hands were as cold as ice when I played outside.

The vanilla pudding is as smooth as silk.

The clouds look like cotton balls in the sky.

The joke was so funny that Adam laughed like a hyena!

Santa's belly is as round as a bowl full of jelly.

My younger brother is as stubborn as a mule.

The lake in the morning looks like a sheet of glass.

The excited girl hopped around like a rabbit.

Ava ran to the store as quick as a wink to get some milk.

We're all in the same boat.

Time flies when you are busy.

The math assignment was a piece of cake.

It's raining cats and dogs out there today!

Dakota had butterflies in her stomach when she sang a solo.

Maggie was under the weather so she stayed home.

Button your lip!

Does the cat have your tongue?

I have a frog in my throat!

Teacher Created Resources

Teacher Created Resources

Teacher Created Resources

Teacher Created Resources

Teacher Created Resources

Teacher Created Resources

Teacher Created Resources

Teacher Created Resources

Teacher Created Resources

Teacher Created Resources

Teacher Created Resources

Teacher Created Resources

Teacher Created Resources

Teacher Created Resources

Teacher Created Resources

Teacher Created Resources

Teacher Created Resources

Teacher Created Resources

Teacher Created Resources

Teacher Created Resources

Teacher Created Resources

Teacher Created Resources

Teacher Created Resources

Teacher Created Resources

Teacher Created Resources

Teacher Created Resources

Teacher Created Resources

Teacher Created Resources

Teacher Created Resources

Teacher Created Resources

Teacher Created Resources

Teacher Created Resources

Teacher Created Resources

Teacher Created Resources

Teacher Created Resources

Teacher Created Resources

Go Figure!

Player B		Player B		Player B		Player B
	metaphor		alliteration		idiom	
simile		idiom		metaphor		simile
	Free Spot		Power Spot		Free Spot	
alliteration		simile		idiom		metaphor
	metaphor		alliteration		simile	
Player A		Player A		Player A		Player A

Teacher Created Resources

Teacher Created Resources

Teacher Created Resources

Teacher Created Resources

Teacher Created Resources

Teacher Created Resources

Teacher Created Resources

Teacher Created Resources

Teacher Created Resources

Teacher Created Resources

Teacher Created Resources

Teacher Created Resources

Teacher Created Resources

Teacher Created Resources

Teacher Created Resources

Teacher Created Resources

Teacher Created Resources

Teacher Created Resources

Teacher Created Resources

Teacher Created Resources

Teacher Created Resources

Teacher Created Resources

Teacher Created Resources

Teacher Created Resources

Teacher Created Resources

Teacher Created Resources

Teacher Created Resources

Teacher Created Resources

Teacher Created Resources

Teacher Created Resources

Teacher Created Resources

Teacher Created Resources

Teacher Created Resources

Teacher Created Resources

40

©Teacher Created Resources, Inc.

Guide Word Swish!

Skill: guide words

Standard: gathers and uses information for research purposes

Benchmark: uses key words, guide words, alphabetical and numerical order, indexes, cross-references, and letters on volumes to find information for research topics

Materials

- Guide Word Swish! game boards
- Guide Word Swish! cards
- a copy of Guide Word Swish! score card sheet for each player
- Guide Word Swish! answer key

Suggested Use

- cooperative groups
- centers
- home connection
- tutorial

Directions (2 players)

1. Players choose a game board and use the cards that go with the corresponding game board. For example, game cards 1 will be used to play with game board 1, or game cards 2 will be used to play with game board 2.
2. Each player chooses a side (basket) of the Guide Word Swish! game board.
3. Cards are placed as a draw pile.
4. Player A draws a card from the Guide Word Swish! card pile and decides which basket (guide words) on the game board the word belongs.
5. If the word is correctly placed, Player A's points are recorded (see "How to score" below) on the score sheet, and it is Player B's turn. If a word does not belong to either basket, it is an air ball and the player gets 1 point. If the word is incorrectly placed, it is a foul and the player gets 0 points.

   How to score:

   word fits in your basket (home basket)—3 points
   word fits in opponent's basket (away basket)—2 points
   word does not fit in any basket (air ball)—1 point
   wrong answer (foul)—0 points
6. Play continues for 10 rounds.

Reminder

<u>Guide words</u> are the words that appear at the top of a dictionary page, showing the first and last words on that page.
Example: join—jump

PLAYER'S NAME	1	2	3	4	5	6	7	8	9	10	Total Points
HOME											
AWAY											

home basket—3 points
away basket—2 points

air ball—1 point
foul—0 points

PLAYER'S NAME	1	2	3	4	5	6	7	8	9	10	Total Points
HOME											
AWAY											

home basket—3 points
away basket—2 points

air ball—1 point
foul—0 points

PLAYER'S NAME	1	2	3	4	5	6	7	8	9	10	Total Points
HOME											
AWAY											

home basket—3 points
away basket—2 points

air ball—1 point
foul—0 points

Teacher Created Resources

Teacher Created Resources

Teacher Created Resources

Teacher Created Resources

Teacher Created Resources

Teacher Created Resources

Teacher Created Resources

Teacher Created Resources

Teacher Created Resources

Teacher Created Resources

Teacher Created Resources

Teacher Created Resources

Teacher Created Resources

Teacher Created Resources

Teacher Created Resources

Teacher Created Resources

Teacher Created Resources

Teacher Created Resources

Teacher Created Resources

Teacher Created Resources

Teacher Created Resources

Teacher Created Resources

Teacher Created Resources

Teacher Created Resources

Teacher Created Resources

Teacher Created Resources

Teacher Created Resources

Teacher Created Resources

Teacher Created Resources

Teacher Created Resources

Teacher Created Resources

Teacher Created Resources

Teacher Created Resources

Teacher Created Resources

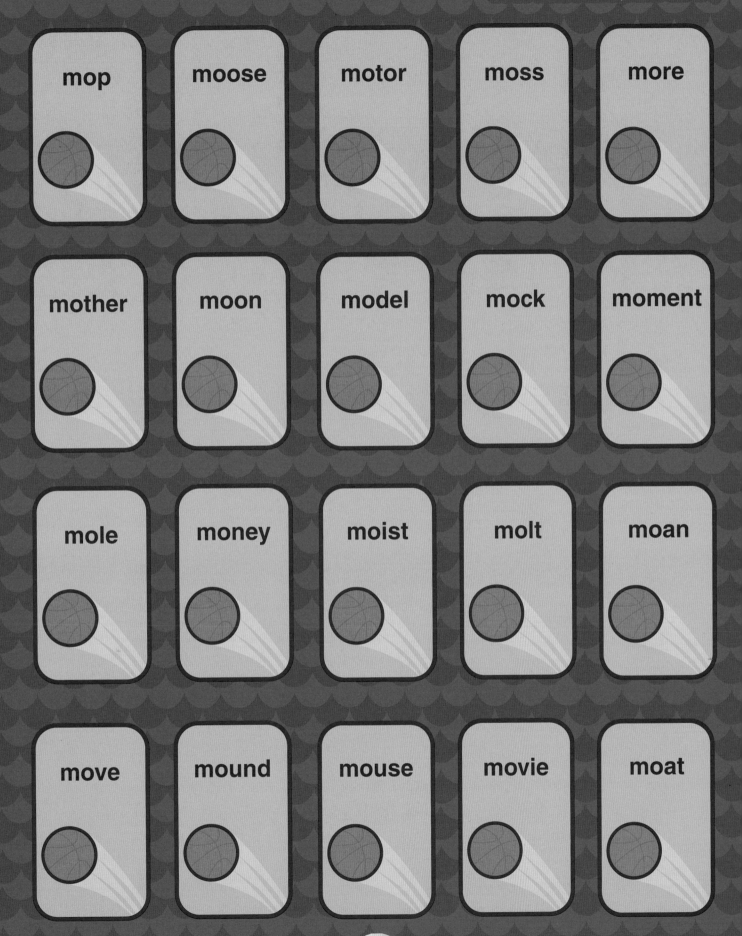

mop

moose

motor

moss

more

mother

moon

model

mock

moment

mole

money

moist

molt

moan

move

mound

mouse

movie

moat

Teacher Created Resources

Teacher Created Resources

Teacher Created Resources

Teacher Created Resources

Teacher Created Resources

Teacher Created Resources

Teacher Created Resources

Teacher Created Resources

Teacher Created Resources

Teacher Created Resources

Teacher Created Resources

Teacher Created Resources

Teacher Created Resources

Teacher Created Resources

Teacher Created Resources

Teacher Created Resources

Teacher Created Resources

Teacher Created Resources

Teacher Created Resources

Teacher Created Resources

Teacher Created Resources

Teacher Created Resources

Teacher Created Resources

Teacher Created Resources

Teacher Created Resources

Teacher Created Resources

Teacher Created Resources

Teacher Created Resources

Teacher Created Resources

Teacher Created Resources

Teacher Created Resources

Teacher Created Resources

Teacher Created Resources

Teacher Created Resources

Teacher Created Resources

Teacher Created Resources

Teacher Created Resources

Teacher Created Resources

Teacher Created Resources

Teacher Created Resources

Teacher Created Resources

Teacher Created Resources

Teacher Created Resources

Teacher Created Resources

Teacher Created Resources

Teacher Created Resources

Teacher Created Resources

Teacher Created Resources

Teacher Created Resources

Teacher Created Resources

Teacher Created Resources

Teacher Created Resources

Teacher Created Resources

Teacher Created Resources

Teacher Created Resources

Teacher Created Resources

Teacher Created Resources

Teacher Created Resources

Teacher Created Resources

Teacher Created Resources

Teacher Created Resources

Teacher Created Resources

Teacher Created Resources

Teacher Created Resources

Teacher Created Resources

Teacher Created Resources

Teacher Created Resources

Teacher Created Resources

Teacher Created Resources

jacket	jam	jaw	jersey	jetty
jewel	jingle	jolly	jot	journal
joy	judge	jug	juice	jog
jungle	junk	jury	just	jute

Teacher Created Resources

Teacher Created Resources

Teacher Created Resources

Teacher Created Resources

Teacher Created Resources

Teacher Created Resources

Teacher Created Resources

Teacher Created Resources

Teacher Created Resources

Teacher Created Resources

Teacher Created Resources

Teacher Created Resources

Teacher Created Resources

Teacher Created Resources

Teacher Created Resources

Teacher Created Resources

Teacher Created Resources

Teacher Created Resources

Teacher Created Resources

Teacher Created Resources

Teacher Created Resources

Teacher Created Resources

Teacher Created Resources

Teacher Created Resources

Teacher Created Resources

Teacher Created Resources

Teacher Created Resources

Teacher Created Resources

Teacher Created Resources

Teacher Created Resources

Teacher Created Resources

Teacher Created Resources

Teacher Created Resources

Teacher Created Resources

Teacher Created Resources

Teacher Created Resources

Teacher Created Resources

51

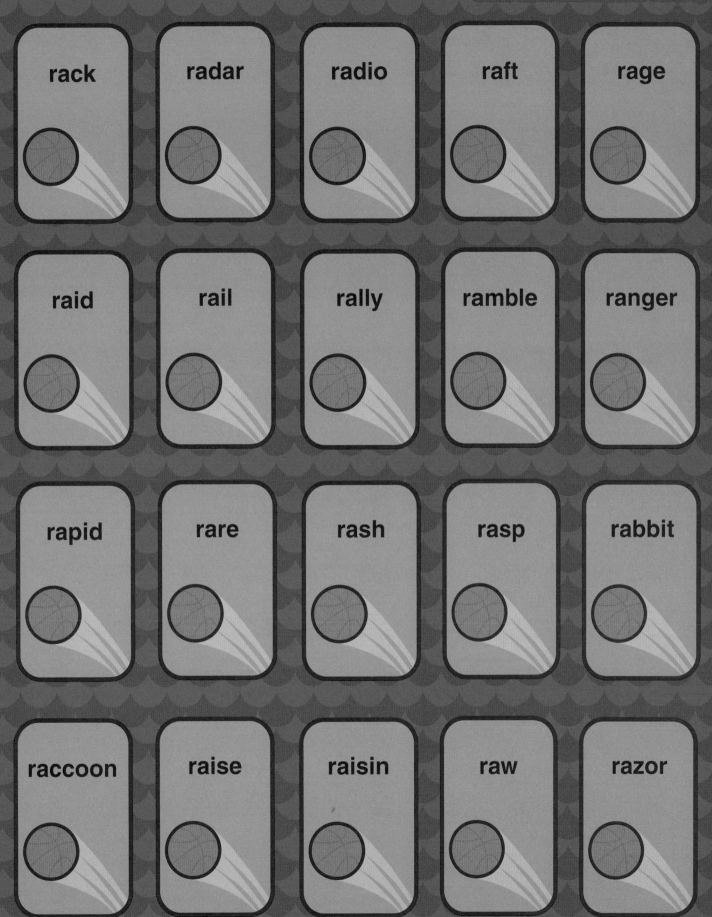

rack

radar

radio

raft

rage

raid

rail

rally

ramble

ranger

rapid

rare

rash

rasp

rabbit

raccoon

raise

raisin

raw

razor

Teacher Created Resources

Teacher Created Resources

Teacher Created Resources

Teacher Created Resources

Teacher Created Resources

Teacher Created Resources

Teacher Created Resources

Teacher Created Resources

Teacher Created Resources

Teacher Created Resources

Teacher Created Resources

Teacher Created Resources

Teacher Created Resources

Teacher Created Resources

Teacher Created Resources

Teacher Created Resources

Teacher Created Resources

Teacher Created Resources

Teacher Created Resources

Teacher Created Resources

Teacher Created Resources

Teacher Created Resources

Teacher Created Resources

Teacher Created Resources

Teacher Created Resources

Teacher Created Resources

Teacher Created Resources

Teacher Created Resources

Teacher Created Resources

Teacher Created Resources

Teacher Created Resources

Teacher Created Resources

Teacher Created Resources

Teacher Created Resources

GUIDE WORD SWISH! ANSWER KEY (Game 1)

moo—motto basket	mob—month basket	no basket
moon	mock	moan
moose	model	moat
mop	moist	mound
more	mole	mouse
moss	molt	move
mother	moment	movie
motor	money	

GUIDE WORD SWISH! ANSWER KEY (Game 2)

jab—job basket	join—jump basket	no basket
jacket	jolly	jog
jam	jot	jungle
jaw	journal	junk
jersey	joy	jury
jetty	judge	just
jewel	jug	jute
jingle	juice	

GUIDE WORD SWISH! ANSWER KEY (Game 3)

race—rain basket	rake—rat basket	no basket
rack	rally	rabbit
radar	ramble	raccoon
radio	ranger	raise
raft	rapid	raisin
rage	rare	raw
raid	rash	razor
rail	rasp	

Teacher Created Resources

Teacher Created Resources

Teacher Created Resources

Teacher Created Resources

Teacher Created Resources

Teacher Created Resources

Teacher Created Resources

Teacher Created Resources

Teacher Created Resources

Teacher Created Resources

Teacher Created Resources

Teacher Created Resources

Teacher Created Resources

Teacher Created Resources

Teacher Created Resources

Teacher Created Resources

Teacher Created Resources

Teacher Created Resources

Teacher Created Resources

Teacher Created Resources

Teacher Created Resources

Teacher Created Resources

Teacher Created Resources

Teacher Created Resources

Teacher Created Resources

Teacher Created Resources

Teacher Created Resources

Teacher Created Resources

Teacher Created Resources

Teacher Created Resources

Teacher Created Resources

Teacher Created Resources

Teacher Created Resources

Teacher Created Resources

Handy Homographs

Skill: homographs

Standard: uses the general skills and strategies for the reading process

Benchmark: understands level-appropriate reading vocabulary (e.g., homographs)

Materials

- Handy Homographs game board
- Handy Homographs playing cards
- Handy Homographs answer key

Suggested Use

- cooperative groups
- centers
- home connection
- tutorial

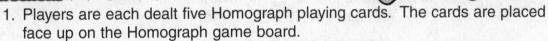

Directions (2 players)

1. Players are each dealt five Homograph playing cards. The cards are placed face up on the Homograph game board.

2. The Homograph cards are placed face up as a draw pile in the center of the Homograph game board. One card is placed face up on the discard pile and read by a player. Each player checks his or her Homograph playing cards for a sentence matching the homograph shown on the Homograph card in the discard pile.

3. The player with the match to the Homograph card takes the top card of the discard pile and matches it with his or her Homograph playing card, setting the match aside.

4. Players continue turning over cards from the draw pile, each player taking the Homograph card that matches his or her card. Any unmatched cards are left in the discard pile.

5. Game continues until one player matches all of his or her Homograph playing cards.

Variation

- The cards can be used as a concentration game.

Reminder

Homographs are words that have the same spelling but different meanings. Sometimes homographs are pronounced differently. Examples: I drank a can of pop. Please don't pop the balloon. A tear ran down her cheek. There is a tear in the paper.

Handy Homographs: Answer Key

Would you like some **pop** with your pizza?
Be careful not to **pop** that balloon.

I **saw** you at the park yesterday.
My dad put the **saw** away in the garage.

Did you bring your ball and **bat** to practice?
The **bat** was flying at night.

I threw the **ball** over the fence!
I am going to wear a gown to the **ball**.

This boat is very difficult to **row**.
Can you see if you sit in the back **row**?

The horses got out of their **pen**.
I bought a new red **pen** at the store.

Make sure to turn off the **light** when you leave.
You may want to wear a **light** jacket.

I saw the birds **fly** over the lake.
That **fly** keeps buzzing around our food.

Please do not **tear** the paper.
Her sad story brought a **tear** to my eye.

I think I **left** my hat here.
Turn **left** at the next corner.

I **dove** into the freezing cold water.
Did you feed the **dove** that was sitting in the tree?

Can you **lead** us back to camp?
I bought a **lead** pencil to use for my homework.

The **wind** was blowing the leaves around.
Make sure to **wind** up the clock before going to bed.

Make sure to **bow** before the king.
She wore a **bow** in her hair for the party.

You need to stand **close** together in line.
Did you remember to **close** the cupboard door?

Did you get to see her perform **live** on stage?
In what town do you **live**?

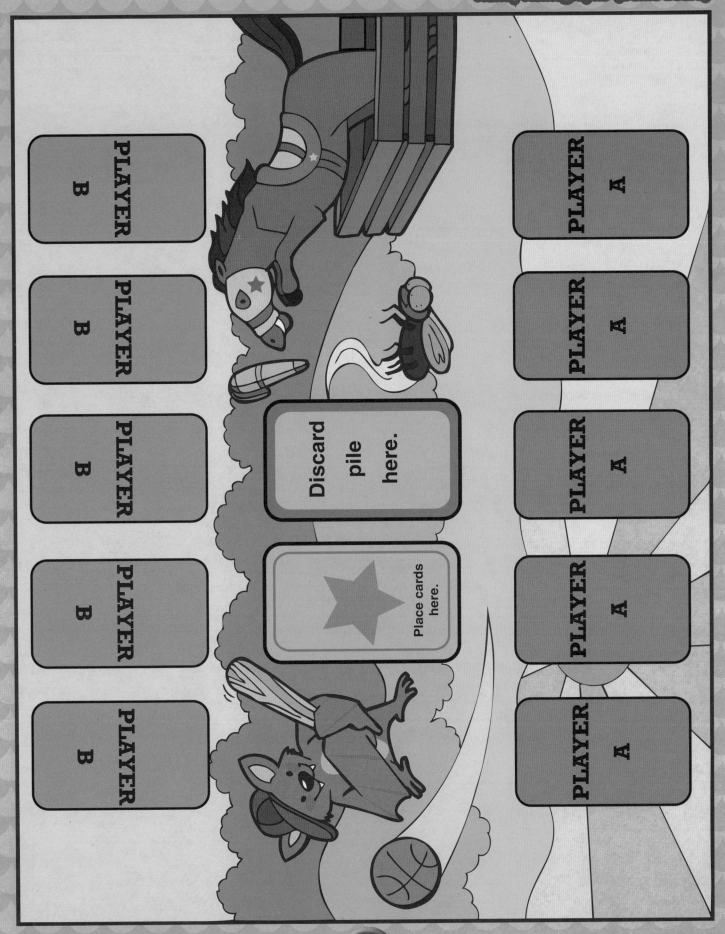

Teacher Created Resources

Teacher Created Resources

Teacher Created Resources

Teacher Created Resources

Teacher Created Resources

Teacher Created Resources

Teacher Created Resources

Teacher Created Resources

Teacher Created Resources

Teacher Created Resources

Teacher Created Resources

Teacher Created Resources

Teacher Created Resources

Teacher Created Resources

Teacher Created Resources

Teacher Created Resources

Teacher Created Resources

Teacher Created Resources

Teacher Created Resources

Teacher Created Resources

Teacher Created Resources

Teacher Created Resources

Teacher Created Resources

Teacher Created Resources

Teacher Created Resources

Teacher Created Resources

Teacher Created Resources

Teacher Created Resources

Teacher Created Resources

Teacher Created Resources

Teacher Created Resources

Teacher Created Resources

Teacher Created Resources

Teacher Created Resources

Teacher Created Resources

Teacher Created Resources

Would you like some **pop** with your pizza?

Be careful not to **pop** the balloon.

I **saw** you at the park yesterday.

My dad put the **saw** away in the garage.

Did you bring your ball and **bat** to practice?

The **bat** was flying at night.

I saw the birds **fly** over the lake.

That **fly** keeps buzzing around our food.

This boat is very difficult to **row**.

Can you see if you sit in the back **row**?

The horses got out of their **pen**.

I bought a new red **pen** at the store.

I threw the **ball** over the fence!

I am going to wear a gown to the **ball**.

Make sure to turn off the **light** when you leave.

You may want to wear a **light** jacket.

Teacher Created Resources

Teacher Created Resources

Teacher Created Resources

Teacher Created Resources

Teacher Created Resources

Teacher Created Resources

Teacher Created Resources

Teacher Created Resources

Teacher Created Resources

Teacher Created Resources

Teacher Created Resources

Teacher Created Resources

Teacher Created Resources

Teacher Created Resources

Teacher Created Resources

Teacher Created Resources

Teacher Created Resources

Teacher Created Resources

Teacher Created Resources

Teacher Created Resources

Teacher Created Resources

Teacher Created Resources

Teacher Created Resources

Teacher Created Resources

Teacher Created Resources

Teacher Created Resources

Teacher Created Resources

Teacher Created Resources

Teacher Created Resources

Teacher Created Resources

Teacher Created Resources

Teacher Created Resources

Teacher Created Resources

Teacher Created Resources

Teacher Created Resources

Please do not **tear** the paper.

Her sad story brought a **tear** to my eye.

The **wind** was blowing the leaves around.

Make sure to **wind** up the clock before going to bed.

I think I **left** my hat here.

Turn **left** at the next corner.

Make sure to **bow** before the king.

She wore a **bow** in her hair for the party.

I **dove** into the freezing cold water.

Did you feed the **dove** that was sitting in the tree?

You need to stand **close** together in line.

Did you remember to **close** the cupboard door?

Can you **lead** us back to camp?

I bought a **lead** pencil to use for my homework.

Did you get to see her perform **live** on stage?

In what town do you **live**?

Teacher Created Resources

Teacher Created Resources

Teacher Created Resources

Teacher Created Resources

Teacher Created Resources

Teacher Created Resources

Teacher Created Resources

Teacher Created Resources

Teacher Created Resources

Teacher Created Resources

Teacher Created Resources

Teacher Created Resources

Teacher Created Resources

Teacher Created Resources

Teacher Created Resources

Teacher Created Resources

Teacher Created Resources

Teacher Created Resources

Teacher Created Resources

Teacher Created Resources

Teacher Created Resources

Teacher Created Resources

Teacher Created Resources

Teacher Created Resources

Teacher Created Resources

Teacher Created Resources

Teacher Created Resources

Teacher Created Resources

Teacher Created Resources

Teacher Created Resources

Teacher Created Resources

Teacher Created Resources

Homophone Tic Tac Toe

Skill: homophones

Standard: uses the general skills and stratagies for the reading process

Benchmark: understands level-appropriate reading vocabulary (e.g., homophones)

Materials

- Homophone Tic Tac Toe game board
- Homophone Tic Tac Toe game markers
- Homophone Tic Tac Toe cards
- Homophone Tic Tac Toe answer key

Suggested Use

- cooperative groups
- centers
- home connection
- tutorial

Directions (2 players)

1. Cut the game markers apart and place the Homophone Tic Tac Toe game board on a flat surface. Place Homophone Tic Tac Toe sentence cards in a draw pile.

2. Player A draws and reads the top card of the draw pile. Player A states the correct homophone to use in the sentence.

3. Player B checks the Homophone Tic Tac Toe answer key for the correct answer. If correct, Player A places a Homophone game marker on the Homophone Tic Tac Toe game board, and the card is placed at the bottom of the draw pile. If the answer given is incorrect, the turn goes to the next player, and the card is placed at the bottom of the draw pile.

4. Play continues until one player gets three in a row or a "Homophone Tic Tac Toe."

Reminder

<u>Homophones</u> are words that sound alike but are spelled differently and have different meanings.
Example: one-won

Homophone Tic Tac Toe: Answer Key

1. one
2. won
3. great
4. grate
5. pear
6. pair
7. too
8. to
9. there
10. their
11. wait
12. weight
13. write
14. right
15. sent

16. cent
17. deer
18. dear
19. sale
20. sail
21. blue
22. blew
23. know
24. no
25. eight
26. ate
27. mane
28. main
29. not
30. knot

Teacher Created Resources

Teacher Created Resources

Teacher Created Resources

Teacher Created Resources

Teacher Created Resources

Teacher Created Resources

Teacher Created Resources

Teacher Created Resources

Teacher Created Resources

Teacher Created Resources

Teacher Created Resources

Teacher Created Resources

Teacher Created Resources

Teacher Created Resources

Teacher Created Resources

Teacher Created Resources

Teacher Created Resources

Teacher Created Resources

Teacher Created Resources

Teacher Created Resources

Teacher Created Resources

Teacher Created Resources

Teacher Created Resources

Teacher Created Resources

Teacher Created Resources

Teacher Created Resources

Teacher Created Resources

Teacher Created Resources

Teacher Created Resources

Teacher Created Resources

Teacher Created Resources

Teacher Created Resources

Teacher Created Resources

Teacher Created Resources

1

I have (**one / won**) cat.

2

Bill's team (**one / won**) the basketball game.

3

That was a (**grate / great**) book.

4

She is going to (**grate / great**) some cheese for the pizza.

5

I am going to have a (**pear / pair**) for a snack.

6

Jill needs a new (**pear / pair**) of running shoes.

7

I am going to the store (**too / to**).

8

We went (**too / to**) the shopping mall yesterday.

9

(**Their / There**) is my school.

10

(**Their / There**) car is the red one.

Teacher Created Resources

Teacher Created Resources

Teacher Created Resources

Teacher Created Resources

Teacher Created Resources

Teacher Created Resources

Teacher Created Resources

Teacher Created Resources

Teacher Created Resources

Teacher Created Resources

Teacher Created Resources

Teacher Created Resources

Teacher Created Resources

Teacher Created Resources

Teacher Created Resources

Teacher Created Resources

Teacher Created Resources

Teacher Created Resources

Teacher Created Resources

Teacher Created Resources

Teacher Created Resources

Teacher Created Resources

Teacher Created Resources

Teacher Created Resources

Teacher Created Resources

Teacher Created Resources

Teacher Created Resources

Teacher Created Resources

Teacher Created Resources

Teacher Created Resources

Teacher Created Resources

Teacher Created Resources

Teacher Created Resources

Teacher Created Resources

11

(**Weight / Wait**) here while I am gone.

12

What is the (**weight / wait**) of the elephant?

13

I like to (**right / write**) poems.

14

Are we going in the (**right / write**) direction?

15

Carl (**sent / cent**) him a letter.

16

I only have one (**sent / cent**) left in my bank!

17

Look at the beautiful (**dear / deer**) in the meadow.

18

My friend is very (**dear / deer**) to me.

19

Paul is having a yard (**sail / sale**) tomorrow.

20

The boat is going to (**sail / sale**) around the lake.

Teacher Created Resources

Teacher Created Resources

Teacher Created Resources

Teacher Created Resources

Teacher Created Resources

Teacher Created Resources

Teacher Created Resources

Teacher Created Resources

Teacher Created Resources

Teacher Created Resources

Teacher Created Resources

Teacher Created Resources

Teacher Created Resources

Teacher Created Resources

Teacher Created Resources

Teacher Created Resources

Teacher Created Resources

Teacher Created Resources

Teacher Created Resources

Teacher Created Resources

Teacher Created Resources

Teacher Created Resources

Teacher Created Resources

Teacher Created Resources

Teacher Created Resources

Teacher Created Resources

Teacher Created Resources

Teacher Created Resources

Teacher Created Resources

Teacher Created Resources

Teacher Created Resources

Teacher Created Resources

Teacher Created Resources

Teacher Created Resources

21

The sky is very
(**blue** / **blew**) today.

22

The wind (**blue** / **blew**)
over the garbage can.

23

Do you (**know** / **no**) the
answer?

24

I have (**know** / **no**)
money left to spend.

25

The spider has
(**ate** / **eight**) legs.

26

Mary (**ate** / **eight**) supper at
her friend's house.

27

The horse's (**main** / **mane**)
is black.

28

What is the (**main** / **mane**)
idea of the story?

29

I am (**not** / **knot**)
able to go with you.

30

Make sure the
(**not** / **knot**) is tight.

Teacher Created Resources

Teacher Created Resources

Teacher Created Resources

Teacher Created Resources

Teacher Created Resources

Teacher Created Resources

Teacher Created Resources

Teacher Created Resources

Teacher Created Resources

Teacher Created Resources

Teacher Created Resources

Teacher Created Resources

Teacher Created Resources

Teacher Created Resources

Teacher Created Resources

Teacher Created Resources

Teacher Created Resources

Teacher Created Resources

Teacher Created Resources

Teacher Created Resources

Teacher Created Resources

Teacher Created Resources

Teacher Created Resources

Teacher Created Resources

Teacher Created Resources

Teacher Created Resources

Teacher Created Resources

Teacher Created Resources

Teacher Created Resources

Teacher Created Resources

Teacher Created Resources

Teacher Created Resources

Teacher Created Resources

Teacher Created Resources

Teacher Created Resources

Teacher Created Resources

©Teacher Created Resources, Inc.

Sentence Show Down

Skill: kinds of sentences

Standard: uses the stylistic and rhetorical aspects of writing

Benchmark: uses a variety of sentence structures in writing

Materials

- Sentence Show Down cards

Suggested Use

- teacher led

Directions (whole group)

1. Teacher chooses five, six or seven students (depending on class size) to stand in front of the room. One of the standing students is selected to be the caller.
2. The caller calls out, "Heads down, thumbs up." All students put their heads down (hiding their eyes) and thumbs up.
3. The selected students walk around the room and tap one other student's thumb. That student puts his or her thumb down.
4. When all students have returned to the front of the room, the caller says, "Heads up, stand up." All students whose thumbs were tapped stand up.
5. The teacher chooses and reads a Sentence Show Down card to each standing student. If the student can correctly identify the kind of sentence (statement, question, command, or exclamation), he or she guesses who tapped his or her thumb. If the student's guess is correct, he or she replaces the student who tapped him or her. If the student's guess is incorrect, the student sits down.
8. Students who are not able to identify the sentence correctly, sit down and it is the next player's turn.
9. When all chosen students have had turns, play continues back at step #2.

Variations

- If a student correctly identifies the kind of sentence, he or she gets two guesses. If the student is incorrect, he or she is allowed one guess.
- Students can write their own sentences.
- Students can work with a partner and take turns reading and identifying the sentences.

Reminder

Statements (declarative) tell something. Statements end with a period. (Example: It is cloudy outside today.)
Questions (interrogative) ask something. Questions end with a question mark. (Example: When does the game start?)
Commands (imperative) give an order or make a request. Commands end with a period. (Example: Go do your homework.)
Exclamations (exclamatory) express a strong feeling. Exclamations end with an exclamation point. (Example: The books are missing!)

Teacher Created Resources

Teacher Created Resources

Teacher Created Resources

Teacher Created Resources

Teacher Created Resources

Teacher Created Resources

Teacher Created Resources

Teacher Created Resources

Teacher Created Resources

Teacher Created Resources

Teacher Created Resources

Teacher Created Resources

Teacher Created Resources

Teacher Created Resources

Teacher Created Resources

Teacher Created Resources

Teacher Created Resources

Teacher Created Resources

Teacher Created Resources

Teacher Created Resources

Teacher Created Resources

Teacher Created Resources

Teacher Created Resources

Teacher Created Resources

Teacher Created Resources

Teacher Created Resources

Teacher Created Resources

Teacher Created Resources

Teacher Created Resources

Teacher Created Resources

Teacher Created Resources

Teacher Created Resources

Wear a jacket when you go outside.

COMMAND

Take a book with you.

COMMAND

Turn off the television.

COMMAND

Write your name neatly on the paper.

COMMAND

Wash your hands before you eat.

COMMAND

Turn right when you reach the stop sign.

COMMAND

Turn left at the end of the block.

COMMAND

Pick up the paper around your desk.

COMMAND

Check the tires before riding your bike.

COMMAND

Teacher Created Resources

Teacher Created Resources

Teacher Created Resources

Teacher Created Resources

Teacher Created Resources

Teacher Created Resources

Teacher Created Resources

Teacher Created Resources

Teacher Created Resources

Teacher Created Resources

Teacher Created Resources

Teacher Created Resources

Teacher Created Resources

Teacher Created Resources

Teacher Created Resources

Teacher Created Resources

Teacher Created Resources

Teacher Created Resources

Teacher Created Resources

Teacher Created Resources

Teacher Created Resources

Teacher Created Resources

Teacher Created Resources

Teacher Created Resources

Teacher Created Resources

Teacher Created Resources

Teacher Created Resources

Teacher Created Resources

Teacher Created Resources

Teacher Created Resources

Teacher Created Resources

Teacher Created Resources

Teacher Created Resources

Teacher Created Resources

Teacher Created Resources

Teacher Created Resources

This is a fun game!

EXCLAMATION

What a fierce roar the lion has!

EXCLAMATION

Run for your life!

EXCLAMATION

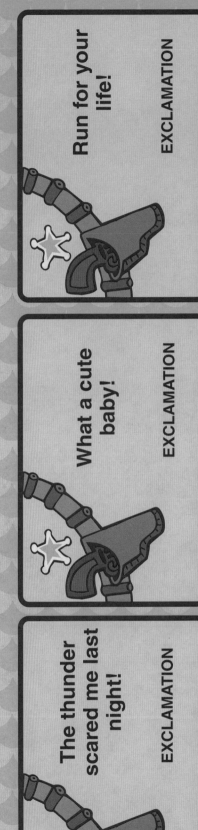

We won the basketball game!

EXCLAMATION

What a nice day!

EXCLAMATION

What a cute baby!

EXCLAMATION

I am so excited about the birthday party!

EXCLAMATION

Help, I can't find my puppy!

EXCLAMATION

The thunder scared me last night!

EXCLAMATION

Teacher Created Resources

Teacher Created Resources

Teacher Created Resources

Teacher Created Resources

Teacher Created Resources

Teacher Created Resources

Teacher Created Resources

Teacher Created Resources

Teacher Created Resources

Teacher Created Resources

Teacher Created Resources

Teacher Created Resources

Teacher Created Resources

Teacher Created Resources

Teacher Created Resources

Teacher Created Resources

Teacher Created Resources

Teacher Created Resources

Teacher Created Resources

Teacher Created Resources

Teacher Created Resources

Teacher Created Resources

Teacher Created Resources

Teacher Created Resources

Teacher Created Resources

Teacher Created Resources

Teacher Created Resources

Teacher Created Resources

Teacher Created Resources

Teacher Created Resources

Teacher Created Resources

Teacher Created Resources

Teacher Created Resources

Teacher Created Resources

Teacher Created Resources

Teacher Created Resources

QUESTION

What are we doing today?

QUESTION

Are the neighbors planting a garden?

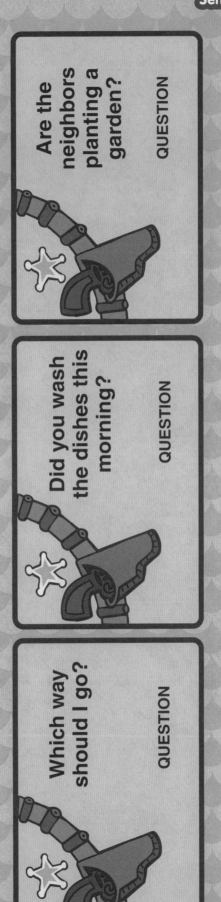

QUESTION

On what page does chapter five begin?

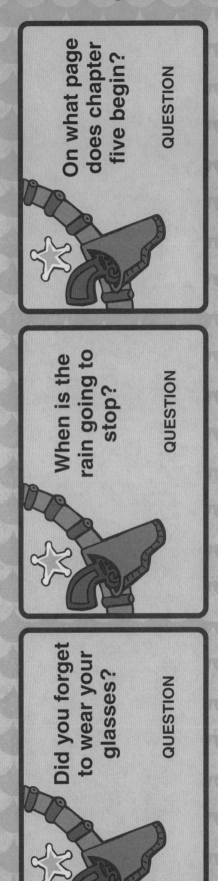

QUESTION

When did you get a new puppy?

QUESTION

Did you wash the dishes this morning?

QUESTION

When is the rain going to stop?

QUESTION

Why were you late for school yesterday?

QUESTION

Which way should I go?

QUESTION

Did you forget to wear your glasses?

Teacher Created Resources

Teacher Created Resources

Teacher Created Resources

Teacher Created Resources

Teacher Created Resources

Teacher Created Resources

Teacher Created Resources

Teacher Created Resources

Teacher Created Resources

Teacher Created Resources

Teacher Created Resources

Teacher Created Resources

Teacher Created Resources

Teacher Created Resources

Teacher Created Resources

Teacher Created Resources

Teacher Created Resources

Teacher Created Resources

Teacher Created Resources

Teacher Created Resources

Teacher Created Resources

Teacher Created Resources

Teacher Created Resources

Teacher Created Resources

Teacher Created Resources

Teacher Created Resources

Teacher Created Resources

Teacher Created Resources

Teacher Created Resources

Teacher Created Resources

Teacher Created Resources

Teacher Created Resources

Teacher Created Resources

Teacher Created Resources

Teacher Created Resources

Teacher Created Resources

My mom read the new book to me last night.

STATEMENT

The phone rang many times.

STATEMENT

My computer was making a funny noise.

STATEMENT

The flowers bloom in the spring.

STATEMENT

The brothers take turns watering the lawn.

STATEMENT

The coins fell to the floor.

STATEMENT

The two cats were sleeping by the window.

STATEMENT

The zoo animals ate their food quickly.

STATEMENT

I like picking green apples from the tree in my backyard.

STATEMENT

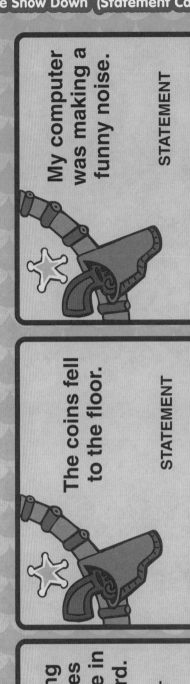

Teacher Created Resources

Teacher Created Resources

Teacher Created Resources

Teacher Created Resources

Teacher Created Resources

Teacher Created Resources

Teacher Created Resources

Teacher Created Resources

Teacher Created Resources

Teacher Created Resources

Teacher Created Resources

Teacher Created Resources

Teacher Created Resources

Teacher Created Resources

Teacher Created Resources

Teacher Created Resources

Teacher Created Resources

Teacher Created Resources

Teacher Created Resources

Teacher Created Resources

Teacher Created Resources

Teacher Created Resources

Teacher Created Resources

Teacher Created Resources

Teacher Created Resources

Teacher Created Resources

Teacher Created Resources

Teacher Created Resources

Teacher Created Resources

Teacher Created Resources

Teacher Created Resources

Teacher Created Resources

Teacher Created Resources

Teacher Created Resources

Teacher Created Resources

Noun Galaxy

Skill: common and proper nouns

Standard: uses grammatical and mechanical conventions in written compositions

Benchmark: uses nouns in written compositions (e.g., uses common and proper nouns)

Materials

- Noun Galaxy game board
- Noun Galaxy sentence cards
- game markers (counters, pennies, or buttons)
- Noun Galaxy answer key

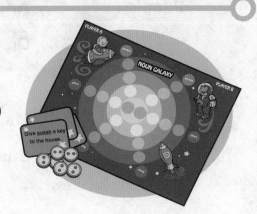

Suggested Use

- cooperative groups
- centers
- home connection
- tutorial

Directions (2 players)

1. Each player chooses a side of the game board and places a game marker on the person, place, and thing circles outside the game planet.

2. Place the Noun Galaxy sentence cards in a draw pile. Player A draws and reads the top card of the draw pile and states if the underlined word or words are common or proper nouns and why. For example, if *friday* is underlined, the player would state, "Friday is a proper noun so it needs to be capitalized."

3. Player B checks the answer key for the correct answer. If correct, Player A moves a game marker in the correct path toward the center of the game for the noun. (Player A would move a marker in the thing column because Friday is a noun that names a thing.) If an incorrect answer is given or the player has completed the path, the turn goes to the next player. The card is then placed at the bottom of the draw pile.

4. Play continues until one player's three game markers are on the middle circle.

Reminder

A <u>noun</u> is a word that stands for a person, place, or thing.
A <u>common noun</u> does not need to begin with a capital letter.
Examples: banker, library, chair
A <u>proper noun</u> is a name given to a specific person, place, or thing.
A proper noun begins with a capital letter.
Examples: Mr. Jones, Texas, January

Noun Galaxy: Answer Key

	PROPER	COMMON
People	Andrew Zinch	artist
	Dr. Smith	friend
	Mr. Olson	librarian
	Ms. Chang	nurse
	Susan	zookeeper
Places	Asia	airport
	Chicago	mall
	Judy's Bakery	museum
	Kansas	park
	Pacific Ocean	theater
Things	April	baseball
	Friday	butterfly
	Frindle	flashlight
	Olympics	bench
	Rover	leaves

PLAYER B

PLAYER A

NOUN GALAXY

person

person

place

place

thing

thing

©Teacher Created Resources, Inc.

#8717 Standards-Based Activities & Games

Teacher Created Resources

Teacher Created Resources

Teacher Created Resources

Teacher Created Resources

Teacher Created Resources

Teacher Created Resources

Teacher Created Resources

Teacher Created Resources

Teacher Created Resources

Teacher Created Resources

Teacher Created Resources

Teacher Created Resources

Teacher Created Resources

Teacher Created Resources

Teacher Created Resources

Teacher Created Resources

Teacher Created Resources

Teacher Created Resources

Teacher Created Resources

Teacher Created Resources

Teacher Created Resources

Teacher Created Resources

Teacher Created Resources

Teacher Created Resources

Teacher Created Resources

Teacher Created Resources

Teacher Created Resources

Teacher Created Resources

Teacher Created Resources

Teacher Created Resources

Teacher Created Resources

Teacher Created Resources

This morning <u>dr. smith</u> took my sister's temperature.

My family and I went snorkeling in the <u>pacific ocean</u>.

Last <u>april</u> we moved into a new house.

Give <u>susan</u> a key to the house.

The new student is from <u>kansas</u>.

Next <u>friday</u> will be my golden birthday.

<u>ms. chang</u> took the students to music.

We bought the cupcakes at <u>judy's bakery</u>.

My brother named the new puppy <u>rover</u>.

<u>andrew zinch</u> is the last student in line.

<u>asia</u> is the largest continent.

I read the book, <u>frindle</u>, over the weekend.

We gave the lost money to <u>mr. olson</u>.

<u>chicago</u> has a lot of tall buildings and people.

The swimmer won a gold medal at the <u>olympics</u>.

Teacher Created Resources

Teacher Created Resources

Teacher Created Resources

Teacher Created Resources

Teacher Created Resources

Teacher Created Resources

Teacher Created Resources

Teacher Created Resources

Teacher Created Resources

Teacher Created Resources

Teacher Created Resources

Teacher Created Resources

Teacher Created Resources

Teacher Created Resources

Teacher Created Resources

Teacher Created Resources

Teacher Created Resources

Teacher Created Resources

Teacher Created Resources

Teacher Created Resources

Teacher Created Resources

Teacher Created Resources

Teacher Created Resources

Teacher Created Resources

Teacher Created Resources

Teacher Created Resources

Teacher Created Resources

Teacher Created Resources

Teacher Created Resources

Teacher Created Resources

Teacher Created Resources

Teacher Created Resources

Teacher Created Resources

Teacher Created Resources

The <u>librarian</u> put the new books on the shelves.

My friends and I went to the <u>theater</u> to see a movie.

The <u>butterfly</u> flew away when it started to rain.

The <u>nurse</u> left the room to get some medicine.

The old <u>museum</u> is filled with colorful paintings.

We needed a <u>flashlight</u> last night when the lights went out.

My new <u>friend</u> came over to ride bikes.

My family went to the <u>mall</u> to shop for school clothes.

The <u>leaves</u> turn brown in autumn.

The angry lion roared at the <u>zookeeper</u>.

Our class stopped at the <u>park</u> for a picnic.

Our old <u>bench</u> needs painting.

The <u>artist</u> painted a picture of the city.

My brother met his friend at the <u>airport</u>.

He hit the <u>baseball</u> over the fence.

Teacher Created Resources

Teacher Created Resources

Teacher Created Resources

Teacher Created Resources

Teacher Created Resources

Teacher Created Resources

Teacher Created Resources

Teacher Created Resources

Teacher Created Resources

Teacher Created Resources

Teacher Created Resources

Teacher Created Resources

Teacher Created Resources

Teacher Created Resources

Teacher Created Resources

Teacher Created Resources

Teacher Created Resources

Teacher Created Resources

Teacher Created Resources

Teacher Created Resources

Teacher Created Resources

Teacher Created Resources

Teacher Created Resources

Teacher Created Resources

Teacher Created Resources

Teacher Created Resources

Teacher Created Resources

Teacher Created Resources

Teacher Created Resources

Teacher Created Resources

Teacher Created Resources

Teacher Created Resources

Teacher Created Resources

Teacher Created Resources

Teacher Created Resources

Teacher Created Resources

92

©Teacher Created Resources, Inc.

Puzzling Possessives

Skill: possessive nouns

Standard: uses grammatical and mechanical conventions in written compositions

Benchmark: uses conventions of punctuation in written compositions (e.g., uses apostrophes in possessive nouns)

Materials

- Puzzling Possessives sentence cards
- a copy of Puzzling Possessives coloring sheet (for each player)
- green, blue, and yellow crayons, markers, or colored pencils

Suggested Use

- cooperative groups
- home connection
- centers
- tutorial

Directions (2 players)

1. Place Puzzling Possessives sentence cards in a draw pile with the sentence side up. Each player receives a Puzzling Possessives coloring sheet.

2. Player A chooses and reads the top card of the draw pile. The player states the correct plural or possessive ending to use in the sentence.

3. Player B checks the back of the card for the correct answer.

4. If correct, Player A colors the matching puzzle piece on the Puzzling Possessives coloring sheet. If the answer given is incorrect or spaces are already colored in, it is the next player's turn.

5. The drawn card is placed at the bottom of the draw pile.

6. Play continues until one player's Puzzling Possessive coloring sheet is completely colored.

Reminder

Possessive nouns are nouns with an added apostrophe and **s** to show ownership.
Examples: dad's hat (singular possessive)
the students' desks (plural possessive)
my three brothers (plural, no possessive)

PUZZLING POSSESSIVES

s = green   's = blue   s' = yellow

94

The **cats** tails are long.

Today we saw the **puffins** nests.

The friend looked for the **girls** bikes.

She moved the **birds** cages.

The **boys** noses were cold.

The **teachers** desks are new.

The three **friends** letters got lost in the mail.

The **babies** beds were all in a row.

Someone lost the **players** uniforms.

The **coaches** whistles were in a drawer.

puffins'   cats'

birds'   girls'

teachers'   boys'

babies'   friends'

coaches'   players'

A **boys** camera is lost.

That **trees** trunk is huge.

A **swimmers** cap is blue.

The **birds** beak is yellow.

The **computers** mouse wasn't working.

We jumped in our **neighbors** boat.

Today is my **dads** birthday.

That **bakers** cake tasted good.

I found a **dogs** leash.

A **schools** flag is missing.

tree's

boy's

bird's

swimmer's

neighbor's

computer's

baker's

dad's

school's

dog's

98

©Teacher Created Resources, Inc.

My **papers** fell to the floor.

Our **flowers** grew tall.

The **streets** are narrow.

The **bears** hid in the cave.

I forgot the **cherries** at home.

The **players** were happy at the end of the game.

The **houses** are the same color.

My **brothers** laughed at the joke.

The **dogs** came running in.

I visited two **schools** today.

99

flowers

papers

bears

streets

players

cherries

brothers

houses

schools

dogs

Word Wizard

Skill: prefixes and suffixes

Standard: uses the general skills and strategies of the reading process

Benchmark: uses phonetic and structural analysis techniques, syntactic structure, and semantic context to decode unknown words (e.g., affixes)

Materials

- a copy of Word Wizard game sheet (for each player)
- corresponding Word Wizard answer key
- colored pencils or markers
- pencil
- die

Suggested Use

- cooperative groups
- centers
- teacher led
- home connection
- tutorial
- independent

Directions (1 to 4 players)

1. Choose a Word Wizard game sheet. Each player needs a copy of the Word Wizard game sheet.
2. Player A rolls the die and finds the column number on the Word Wizard game sheet corresponding with the number on the die. (If a six is rolled, the player can choose any of the 5 columns.) Player A then chooses a base word from the column and a suffix or prefix from the Word Wizard Box to form a correct word. Player A states the word aloud.
3. Player B checks the word on the corresponding Word Wizard answer key. If correct, Player A completes the word on the game sheet and colors the Wizard's hat next to the word. If incorrect, Player A does not complete the word on the game sheet, and it is Player B's turn.
4. Play continues until one player has colored in all three Wizards' hats in a column.

Variations

- The teacher can determine the number of words written and colored in on the game sheet.
- Students can use game pieces to cover the answers.

Reminder

An <u>affix</u> is a part of a word that is added on to a base or root word.
- *prefix* = a part of a word that is added on to the beginning of a base or root word
  Example: <u>un</u>happy, <u>re</u>read, <u>mis</u>understood
- *suffix* = a part of a word that is added on to the end of a base or root word
  Example: care<u>less</u>, slow<u>ly</u>, walk<u>ing</u>

Teacher
Created
Resources

Teacher
Created
Resources

Teacher
Created
Resources

Teacher
Created
Resources

Teacher
Created
Resources

Teacher
Created
Resources

Teacher
Created
Resources

Teacher
Created
Resources

Teacher
Created
Resources

Teacher
Created
Resources

Teacher
Created
Resources

Teacher
Created
Resources

Teacher
Created
Resources

Teacher
Created
Resources

Teacher
Created
Resources

Teacher
Created
Resources

Teacher
Created
Resources

Teacher
Created
Resources

Teacher
Created
Resources

Teacher
Created
Resources

Teacher
Created
Resources

Teacher
Created
Resources

Teacher
Created
Resources

Teacher
Created
Resources

Teacher
Created
Resources

Teacher
Created
Resources

Teacher
Created
Resources

Teacher
Created
Resources

Teacher
Created
Resources

Teacher
Created
Resources

Teacher
Created
Resources

Teacher
Created
Resources

Teacher
Created
Resources

Teacher
Created
Resources

Teacher
Created
Resources

Teacher
Created
Resources

WORD WIZARD

WORD WIZARD

Answer Key

Word Wizard Box

–er   –less   –ful

1	jumper	homeless	fruitless / fruitful
2	handful	powerless / powerful	teacher
3	driver	helper / helpless / helpful	restless / restful
4	careless / careful	farmer	sleeper / sleepless
5	fearless / fearful	timer / timeless	roomer / roomful

5

select ___

great ___

throw ___

4

sad ___

crawl ___

friend ___

3

watch ___

slow ___

smooth ___

2

quick ___

light ___

warm ___

1

sick ___

laugh ___

kind ___

Word Wizard Box

–ness

–ly

–ing

WORD WIZARD

Answer Key

WORD-WIZARD

Word Wizard Box

–ing   –ly   –ness

1
- sickly
- sickness
- laughing
- kindly
- kindness

2
- quickly
- quickness
- lighting
- lightly
- lightness
- warming
- warmly

3
- watching
- slowing
- slowly
- smoothing
- smoothly
- smoothness

4
- sadly
- sadness
- crawling
- friendly

5
- selecting
- selectness
- greatly
- greatness
- throwing

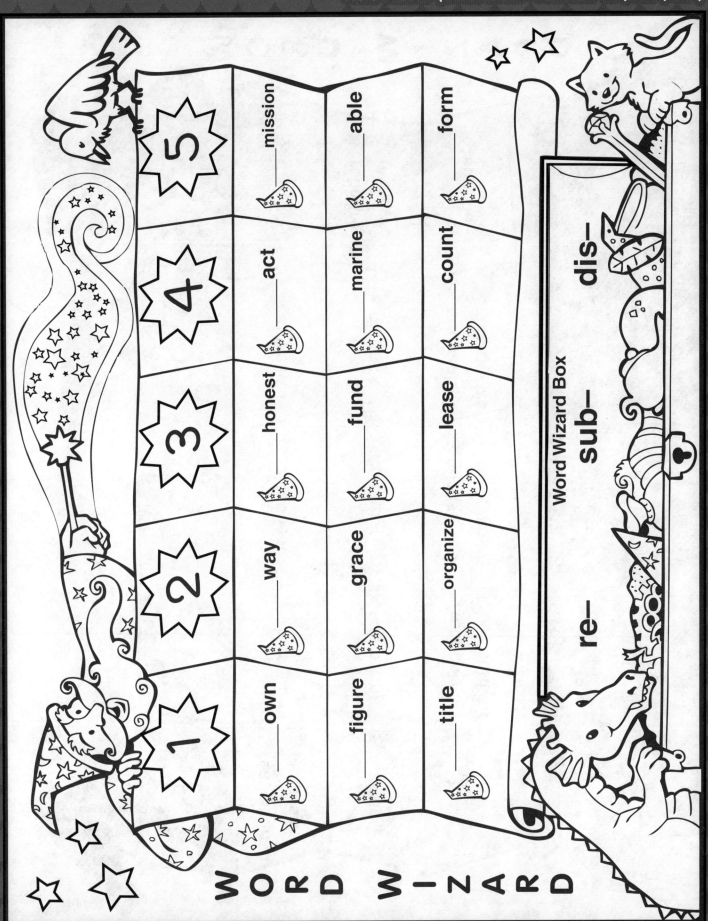

5 — mission
5 — able
5 — form

4 — act
4 — marine
4 — count

3 — honest
3 — fund
3 — lease

2 — way
2 — grace
2 — organize

1 — own
1 — figure
1 — title

Word Wizard Box

re– sub– dis–

WORD WIZARD

WORD WIZARD

Answer Key

1	2	3	4	5
disown	subway	dishonest	react	remission submission
refigure	disgrace	refund	submarine	disable
disfigure				
subtitle	reorganize	release	recount	reform
	disorganize	sublease	discount	

Word Wizard Box

re–   sub–   dis–

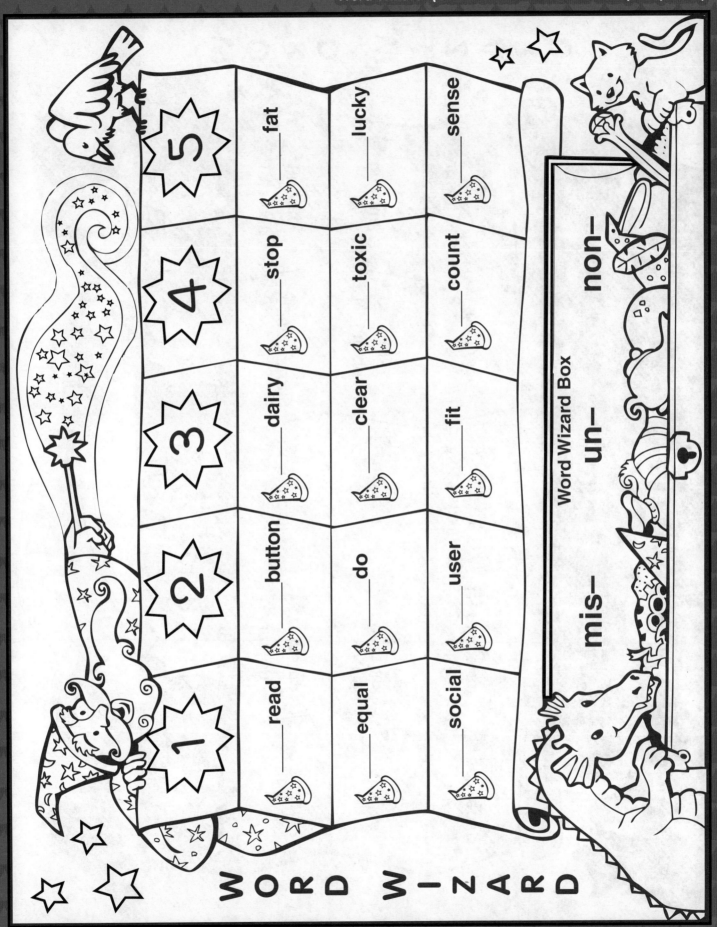

Word Wizard Box

non–

un–

mis–

WORD WIZARD

5	4	3	2	1
____ fat	____ stop	____ dairy	____ button	____ read
____ lucky	____ toxic	____ clear	____ do	____ equal
____ sense	____ count	____ fit	____ user	____ social

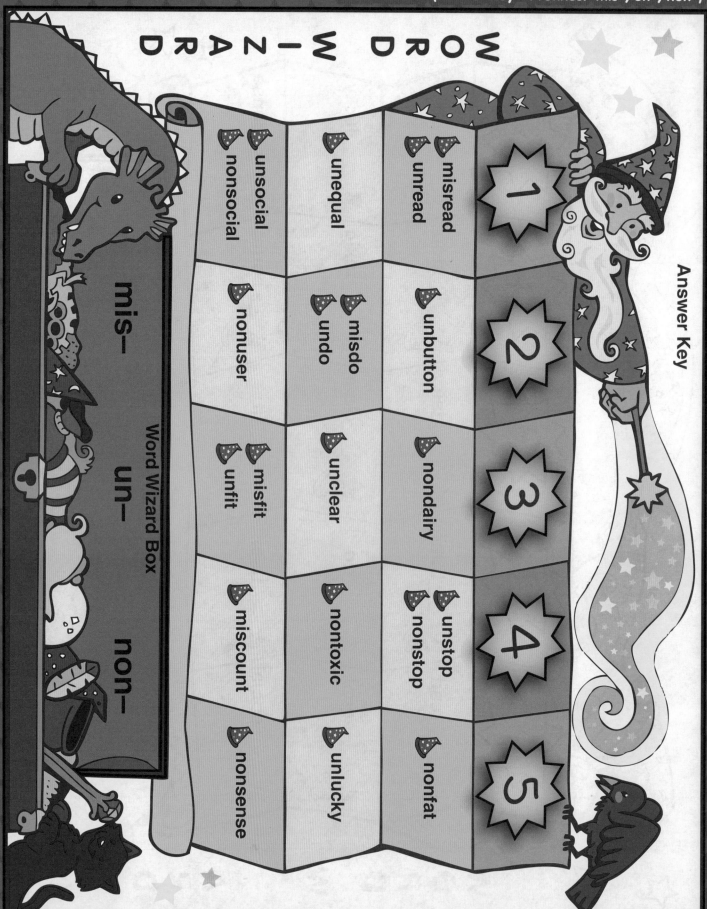

Answer Key

WORD W-IZARD

Word Wizard Box

mis– un– non–

1	misread / unread	unequal	unsocial / nonsocial
2	unbutton	misdo / undo	nonuser
3	nondairy	unclear	misfit / unfit
4	unstop / nonstop	nontoxic	miscount
5	nonfat	unlucky	nonsense

©Teacher Created Resources, Inc.

Pronoun Pizzazz

Skill: objective and subjective pronouns

Standard: uses grammatical and mechanical conventions in writing

Benchmark: uses pronouns in written compositions

Materials

- a copy of Pronoun Pizzazz game board (for each player)
- Pronoun Pizzazz game cards
- Pronoun Pizzazz answer key
- game markers (chips, pennies, or buttons)

Suggested Use

- cooperative groups
- home connection
- centers
- tutorial

Directions (2–4 players)

1. Each player receives a Pronoun Pizzazz game board.

2. Place Pronoun Pizzazz game cards in a draw pile between the players.

3. Player A chooses and reads the top card of the draw pile. The player states the correct pronoun to replace the underlined part of the sentence.

4. Player B checks the answer key for the correct answer. If correct, Player A places a game marker on the matching star on the Pronoun Pizzazz game board. The card is placed at the bottom of the draw pile. If the answer given is incorrect or the space is already covered, the turn goes to the next player. The card is then placed at the bottom of the draw pile.

5. Play continues until one player's game board is completely covered with game markers.

Variation

- Players or teacher can determine the winning game pattern (i.e., three in a row, 4 corners, etc.).

Reminder

A <u>subjective pronoun</u> is a replacement word for a noun and acts as the subject of a sentence.
Examples: he, she, we, they, I, it, you
An <u>objective pronoun</u> is a replacement word for a noun and acts as the object of a sentence.
Examples: him, her, us, them, me, it, you

Pronoun Pizzazz: Answer Key

1. he
2. they
3. it
4. them
5. she
6. him
7. we
8. her
9. us
10. she
11. he
12. them
13. we
14. it
15. they
16. her

17. us
18. him
19. we
20. them
21. it
22. us
23. she
24. him
25. they
26. he
27. her
28. it
29. they
30. us
31. him
32. she

Pronoun Pizzazz

he

it

them

they

us

her

we

she

him

Teacher Created Resources

Teacher Created Resources

Teacher Created Resources

Teacher Created Resources

Teacher Created Resources

Teacher Created Resources

Teacher Created Resources

Teacher Created Resources

Teacher Created Resources

Teacher Created Resources

Teacher Created Resources

Teacher Created Resources

Teacher Created Resources

Teacher Created Resources

Teacher Created Resources

Teacher Created Resources

Teacher Created Resources

Teacher Created Resources

Teacher Created Resources

Teacher Created Resources

Teacher Created Resources

Teacher Created Resources

Teacher Created Resources

Teacher Created Resources

Teacher Created Resources

Teacher Created Resources

Teacher Created Resources

Teacher Created Resources

Teacher Created Resources

Teacher Created Resources

Teacher Created Resources

Teacher Created Resources

Teacher Created Resources

Teacher Created Resources

Teacher Created Resources

Teacher Created Resources

Mike rode his new bike to school yesterday.

1

My neighbors left on a bus to the airport.

2

Quickly return **the book** to the library.

3

My sister showed **Mia and Ann** her coin collection.

4

Tomorrow **my aunt** is leaving on a trip to Mexico.

5

Give the tickets to **Tyler** before you leave.

6

Mary and I explained the game to the class.

7

Kim showed **Andrea** how to climb.

8

116

©Teacher Created Resources, Inc.

My uncle will visit **my brothers and me** next summer.

9

Susan drew a picture of an alligator swimming in a river.

10

Only **my brother** knows where the key to the house is hidden.

11

Jonas puts **the oranges** in a paper bag.

12

Last summer **my family and I** visited the city zoo.

13

Megan threw **the ball** over the fence.

14

The players won the game by two points.

15

My mom wants me to go to the parade with **Kay**.

16

Teacher Created Resources

Teacher Created Resources

Teacher Created Resources

Teacher Created Resources

Teacher Created Resources

Teacher Created Resources

Teacher Created Resources

Teacher Created Resources

Teacher Created Resources

Teacher Created Resources

Teacher Created Resources

Teacher Created Resources

Teacher Created Resources

Teacher Created Resources

Teacher Created Resources

Teacher Created Resources

Teacher Created Resources

Teacher Created Resources

Teacher Created Resources

Teacher Created Resources

Teacher Created Resources

Teacher Created Resources

Teacher Created Resources

Teacher Created Resources

Teacher Created Resources

Teacher Created Resources

Teacher Created Resources

Teacher Created Resources

Teacher Created Resources

Teacher Created Resources

Teacher Created Resources

Teacher Created Resources

Teacher Created Resources

Teacher Created Resources

Teacher Created Resources

Teacher Created Resources

Teacher Created Resources

Teacher Created Resources

Teacher Created Resources

Dakota watched the scary movie with **Ethan and me**.

17

I walked to the park with **my big brother**.

18

On Saturday **my friends and I** left the game early.

19

Ava is telling **Maggie and Jill** about the new game she bought.

20

The toy airplane landed in our backyard.

21

Jordan marched in the parade with **Adam and me**.

22

This morning **my sister** watered the vegetables in the garden.

23

Jenny tries to tag **Tyler** with the ball.

24

Teacher Created Resources

Teacher Created Resources

Teacher Created Resources

Teacher Created Resources

Teacher Created Resources

Teacher Created Resources

Teacher Created Resources

Teacher Created Resources

Teacher Created Resources

Teacher Created Resources

Teacher Created Resources

Teacher Created Resources

Teacher Created Resources

Teacher Created Resources

Teacher Created Resources

Teacher Created Resources

Teacher Created Resources

Teacher Created Resources

Teacher Created Resources

Teacher Created Resources

Teacher Created Resources

Teacher Created Resources

Teacher Created Resources

Teacher Created Resources

Teacher Created Resources

Teacher Created Resources

Teacher Created Resources

Teacher Created Resources

Teacher Created Resources

Teacher Created Resources

Teacher Created Resources

Teacher Created Resources

Teacher Created Resources

Teacher Created Resources

Teacher Created Resources

Teacher Created Resources

The twins received birthday cards from their friends.

25

Mr. Andrews coached the winning team.

26

The teacher gave the book about cheetahs to **Marie**.

27

The plant needs to be watered soon.

28

The students wanted more red paper for the art project.

29

After school the teacher showed **Kelly and me** how to do the problem.

30

Dominic invited **Kyle** to the zoo.

31

Finally, **Natasha** found the missing puppy.

32

Teacher Created Resources

Teacher Created Resources

Teacher Created Resources

Teacher Created Resources

Teacher Created Resources

Teacher Created Resources

Teacher Created Resources

Teacher Created Resources

Teacher Created Resources

Teacher Created Resources

Teacher Created Resources

Teacher Created Resources

Teacher Created Resources

Teacher Created Resources

Teacher Created Resources

Teacher Created Resources

Teacher Created Resources

Teacher Created Resources

Teacher Created Resources

Teacher Created Resources

Teacher Created Resources

Teacher Created Resources

Teacher Created Resources

Teacher Created Resources

Teacher Created Resources

Teacher Created Resources

Teacher Created Resources

Teacher Created Resources

Teacher Created Resources

Teacher Created Resources

Teacher Created Resources

Teacher Created Resources

Teacher Created Resources

Teacher Created Resources

Teacher Created Resources

Teacher Created Resources

Diamonds and Dots

Skill: subject and predicate of a sentence

Standard: uses the stylistic and rhetorical aspects of writing

Benchmark: uses a variety of sentence structures in writing

Materials

- Diamonds and Dots game boards
- Diamonds and Dots subject and predicate cards
- Diamonds and Dots answer key
- 2 game markers per player (buttons, chips, etc.)

Suggested Use

- cooperative groups
- home connection
- centers
- tutorial

Directions (2 to 4 players)

1. Each player chooses a player board and places a game marker in each start box.

2. Subject and predicate cards are placed face down in the middle of players as a draw pile. Player A draws a card and reads the sentence. If the card has **S**, the player states the subject of the sentence. If the card has **P**, the player states the predicate of the sentence. If correct, Player A moves a game piece to the first diamond (subject) or dot (predicate) space, and it is the next player's turn. If incorrect or a player cannot move, it is the next player's turn. (*Note:* Some cards will have directions to Skip A Turn, Go Back To Start, etc. instead of a sentence.)

3. Play continues until one player's two game pieces are on the top shapes on the player board.

Reminder

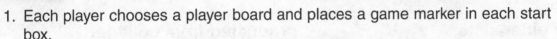

<u>Subject</u> is the part of the sentence that tells what or whom the sentence is about.
Example: <u>The new neighbors</u> seemed friendly.
<u>Predicate</u> is the part of the sentence that tells something about the subject.
Example: The new neighbors <u>seemed friendly</u>.

Diamonds and Dots: Answer Key

SUBJECT	PREDICATE
The small boy	went home early.
They	knew the game would last a long time.
Most dictionaries	are large.
The orange paint	added color to the picture.
All the neighbors	grew tomatoes.
The wild horse	ran away yesterday.
My older sister	graduated from college.
The antique chair	needed a new cushion.
Many students	read the new book.
Some soccer players	stayed after the game to practice.
The new restaurant	has many food choices.
Both fruits and vegetables	should be eaten every day.

Diamonds and Dots

Diamonds and Dots

START (subject)

START (predicate)

START (subject)

START (predicate)

Teacher Created Resources

Teacher Created Resources

Teacher Created Resources

Teacher Created Resources

Teacher Created Resources

Teacher Created Resources

Teacher Created Resources

Teacher Created Resources

Teacher Created Resources

Teacher Created Resources

Teacher Created Resources

Teacher Created Resources

Teacher Created Resources

Teacher Created Resources

Teacher Created Resources

Teacher Created Resources

Teacher Created Resources

Teacher Created Resources

Teacher Created Resources

Teacher Created Resources

Teacher Created Resources

Teacher Created Resources

Teacher Created Resources

Teacher Created Resources

Teacher Created Resources

Teacher Created Resources

Teacher Created Resources

Teacher Created Resources

Teacher Created Resources

Teacher Created Resources

Teacher Created Resources

Teacher Created Resources

Teacher Created Resources

Teacher Created Resources

Teacher Created Resources

Diamonds and Dots

Diamonds and Dots

START
(subject)

START
(predicate)

START
(subject)

START
(predicate)

Teacher Created Resources

Teacher Created Resources

Teacher Created Resources

Teacher Created Resources

Teacher Created Resources

Teacher Created Resources

Teacher Created Resources

Teacher Created Resources

Teacher Created Resources

Teacher Created Resources

Teacher Created Resources

Teacher Created Resources

Teacher Created Resources

Teacher Created Resources

Teacher Created Resources

Teacher Created Resources

Teacher Created Resources

Teacher Created Resources

Teacher Created Resources

Teacher Created Resources

Teacher Created Resources

Teacher Created Resources

Teacher Created Resources

Teacher Created Resources

Teacher Created Resources

Teacher Created Resources

Teacher Created Resources

Teacher Created Resources

Teacher Created Resources

Teacher Created Resources

Teacher Created Resources

Teacher Created Resources

Teacher Created Resources

Teacher Created Resources

Teacher Created Resources

Teacher Created Resources

The small boy went home early.

They knew the game would last a long time.

Most dictionaries are large.

The orange paint added color to the picture.

All the neighbors grew tomatoes.

The wild horse ran away yesterday.

My older sister graduated from college.

The antique chair needed a new cushion.

Many students read the new book.

Some soccer players stayed after the game to practice.

The new restaurant has many food choices.

Both fruits and vegetables should be eaten every day.

SKIP A TURN

GO BACK 2 SPACES

GO BACK TO START

GO BACK 1 SPACE

Teacher Created Resources

Teacher Created Resources

Teacher Created Resources

Teacher Created Resources

Teacher Created Resources

Teacher Created Resources

Teacher Created Resources

Teacher Created Resources

Teacher Created Resources

Teacher Created Resources

Teacher Created Resources

Teacher Created Resources

Teacher Created Resources

Teacher Created Resources

Teacher Created Resources

Teacher Created Resources

Teacher Created Resources

Teacher Created Resources

Teacher Created Resources

Teacher Created Resources

Teacher Created Resources

Teacher Created Resources

Teacher Created Resources

Teacher Created Resources

Teacher Created Resources

Teacher Created Resources

Teacher Created Resources

Teacher Created Resources

Teacher Created Resources

Teacher Created Resources

Teacher Created Resources

Teacher Created Resources

Teacher Created Resources

Teacher Created Resources

Teacher Created Resources

The small boy went home early.

They knew the game would last a long time.

Most dictionaries are large.

The orange paint added color to the picture.

All the neighbors grew tomatoes.

The wild horse ran away yesterday.

My older sister graduated from college.

The antique chair needed a new cushion.

Many students read the new book.

Some soccer players stayed after the game to practice.

The new restaurant has many food choices.

Both fruits and vegetables should be eaten every day.

SKIP A TURN

GO BACK 2 SPACES

GO BACK TO START

GO BACK 1 SPACE

Teacher Created Resources

Teacher Created Resources

Teacher Created Resources

Teacher Created Resources

Teacher Created Resources

Teacher Created Resources

Teacher Created Resources

Teacher Created Resources

Teacher Created Resources

Teacher Created Resources

Teacher Created Resources

Teacher Created Resources

Teacher Created Resources

Teacher Created Resources

Teacher Created Resources

Teacher Created Resources

Teacher Created Resources

Teacher Created Resources

Teacher Created Resources

Teacher Created Resources

Teacher Created Resources

Teacher Created Resources

Teacher Created Resources

Teacher Created Resources

Teacher Created Resources

Teacher Created Resources

Teacher Created Resources

Teacher Created Resources

Teacher Created Resources

Teacher Created Resources

Teacher Created Resources

Teacher Created Resources

Teacher Created Resources

Teacher Created Resources

Synonym Rolls Match-Up

Skill: synonyms

Standard: uses the general skills and strategies of the reading process

Benchmark: understands level-appropriate reading vocabulary (e.g., synonyms)

Materials
- Synonym Rolls Match-Up cards
- Synonym Rolls Match-Up answer key

Suggested Use
- teacher led

Directions (whole class)

1. Teacher distributes a Synonym Rolls Match-Up card to each student.

2. At the teacher's prompt, students move around the room until they find another student with a synonym match.

3. Students lock arms or sit down to indicate a match.

4. When all students have made a match, the teacher checks the matches and collects the cards.

5. The cards are then redistributed to students to play another round.

Variations
- Teacher times the students to see how fast the matches are made.
- Students can walk around trading cards as they pass other students until the teacher prompts them to find their match.

Reminder

<u>Synonyms</u> are words that mean the same or almost the same as other words.
Example: late-tardy

Synomym Rolls Match-Up: Answer Key

fight—feud

neat—tidy

big—large

small—tiny

pause—stop

present—gift

many—several

fix—repair

shore—beach

fast—quick

throw—toss

thin—slim

mad—angry

hurt—injure

insect—bug

home—house

detest—hate

scared—afraid

fight

feud

neat

tidy

big

large

small

tiny

pause

Synonym Rolls

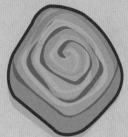

Match-Up

Synonym Rolls

Match-Up

Synonym Rolls

Match-Up

Synonym Rolls

Match-Up

Synonym Rolls

Match-Up

Synonym Rolls

Match-Up

Synonym Rolls

Match-Up

Synonym Rolls

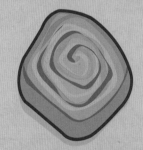

Match-Up

Synonym Rolls

Match-Up

stop

present

gift

many

several

fix

repair

shore

beach

Synonym Rolls

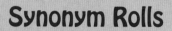

Match-Up

Synonym Rolls

Match-Up

Synonym Rolls

Match-Up

Synonym Rolls

Match-Up

Synonym Rolls

Match-Up

Synonym Rolls

Match-Up

Synonym Rolls

Match-Up

Synonym Rolls

Match-Up

Synonym Rolls

Match-Up

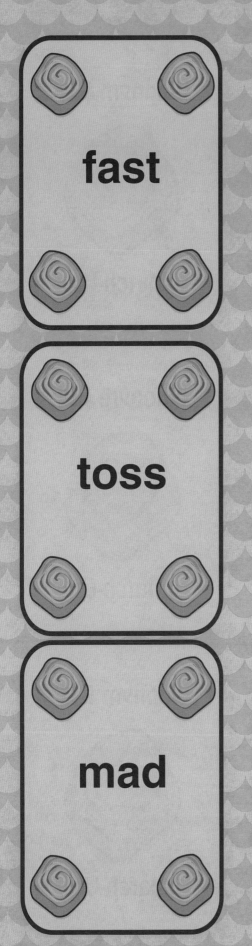

fast

quick

throw

toss

thin

slim

mad

angry

hurt

Synonym Rolls

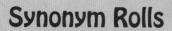

Match-Up

Synonym Rolls

Match-Up

Synonym Rolls

Match-Up

Synonym Rolls

Match-Up

Synonym Rolls

Match-Up

Synonym Rolls

Match-Up

Synonym Rolls

Match-Up

Synonym Rolls

Match-Up

Synonym Rolls

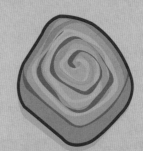

Match-Up

injure

insect

bug

home

house

detest

hate

scared

afraid

Synonym Rolls

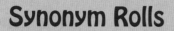

Match-Up

Synonym Rolls

Match-Up

Synonym Rolls

Match-Up

Synonym Rolls

Match-Up

Synonym Rolls

Match-Up

Synonym Rolls

Match-Up

Synonym Rolls

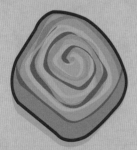

Match-Up

Synonym Rolls

Match-Up

Synonym Rolls

Match-Up

Get Smart

Skill: syllabication

Standard: uses the general skills and strategies of the reading process

Benchmark: uses phonetic and structural analysis techniques, syntactic structure, and semantic context to decode words (e.g., syllabication)

Materials

- Get Smart game board
- Get Smart playing cards
- Get Smart answer key
- game markers (buttons, chips, etc.)

Suggested Use

- cooperative groups
- centers
- home connection
- tutorial

Directions (2 players)

1. Place the Get Smart game board between players and place Get Smart playing cards face down on the game board.

2. Each player places a marker on the Begin arrow.

3. Player A draws the top card from the pile, reads the word aloud and states the number of syllables in the word. Player B checks the answer key. If correct, Player A advances the number of syllables in the word on the Get Smart game board. For example, if the chosen card has two syllables, the player advances two spaces. If the answer is incorrect, Player A stays on the same spot on the game board. The drawn card is returned to the bottom of the draw pile.

4. It is then Player B's turn.

5. Game ends when a player reaches the end of the game board path.

Reminder

Syllabication is the method of dividing words into parts.
Example: ta-ble

Get Smart: Answer Key

One Syllable Cards

1—friend
4—bay
7—spring
8—tooth
10—shook
13—chew
15—leaf
16—spare
19—smile
20—right
22—learn
25—guess
26—crew
30—crowd
58—match

Two Syllable Cards

2—voyage
3—ocean
9—answer
12—captain
18—weather
24—whistle
27—frozen
28—siren
33—second
37—clever
40—because
42—empty
43—mission
45—happy
57—waitress

Three Syllable Cards

5—enjoying
6—directly
11—remember
14—customer
21—example
29—decision
34—finally
35—yesterday
38—silently
41—several
46—animal
50—officer
52—rescuer
53—potato
59—overhead

Four Syllable Cards

17—education
23—impassable
31—definition
32—information
36—cemetery
39—February
44—everyone
47—interesting
48—decorative
49—dictionary
51—impossible
54—January
55—analysis
56—uninhabit
60—illustration

Teacher Created Resources
Teacher Created Resources
Teacher Created Resources
Teacher Created Resources

Teacher Created Resources
Teacher Created Resources
Teacher Created Resources

Teacher Created Resources
Teacher Created Resources
Teacher Created Resources
Teacher Created Resources

Teacher Created Resources
Teacher Created Resources
Teacher Created Resources

Teacher Created Resources
Teacher Created Resources
Teacher Created Resources
Teacher Created Resources

Teacher Created Resources
Teacher Created Resources
Teacher Created Resources

Teacher Created Resources
Teacher Created Resources
Teacher Created Resources
Teacher Created Resources

Teacher Created Resources
Teacher Created Resources
Teacher Created Resources

Teacher Created Resources
Teacher Created Resources
Teacher Created Resources
Teacher Created Resources

friend 1	**bay** 4	**spring** 7
tooth 8	**shook** 10	**chew** 13
leaf 15	**spare** 16	**smile** 19
right 20	**learn** 22	**guess** 25
crew 26	**crowd** 30	**match** 58

Teacher Created Resources

Teacher Created Resources

Teacher Created Resources

Teacher Created Resources

Teacher Created Resources

Teacher Created Resources

Teacher Created Resources

Teacher Created Resources

Teacher Created Resources

Teacher Created Resources

Teacher Created Resources

Teacher Created Resources

Teacher Created Resources

Teacher Created Resources

Teacher Created Resources

Teacher Created Resources

Teacher Created Resources

Teacher Created Resources

Teacher Created Resources

Teacher Created Resources

Teacher Created Resources

Teacher Created Resources

Teacher Created Resources

Teacher Created Resources

Teacher Created Resources

Teacher Created Resources

Teacher Created Resources

Teacher Created Resources

Teacher Created Resources

Teacher Created Resources

Teacher Created Resources

Teacher Created Resources

Teacher Created Resources

Teacher Created Resources

voyage 2	**ocean** 3	**answer** 9
captain 12	**weather** 18	**whistle** 24
frozen 27	**siren** 28	**second** 33
clever 37	**because** 40	**empty** 42
mission 43	**happy** 45	**waitress** 57

Teacher Created Resources

Teacher Created Resources

Teacher Created Resources

Teacher Created Resources

Teacher Created Resources

Teacher Created Resources

Teacher Created Resources

Teacher Created Resources

Teacher Created Resources

Teacher Created Resources

Teacher Created Resources

Teacher Created Resources

Teacher Created Resources

Teacher Created Resources

Teacher Created Resources

Teacher Created Resources

Teacher Created Resources

Teacher Created Resources

Teacher Created Resources

Teacher Created Resources

Teacher Created Resources

Teacher Created Resources

Teacher Created Resources

Teacher Created Resources

Teacher Created Resources

Teacher Created Resources

Teacher Created Resources

Teacher Created Resources

Teacher Created Resources

Teacher Created Resources

Teacher Created Resources

Teacher Created Resources

Teacher Created Resources

Teacher Created Resources

enjoying 5	**directly** 6	**remember** 11
customer 14	**example** 21	**decision** 29
finally 34	**yesterday** 35	**silently** 38
several 41	**animal** 46	**officer** 50
rescuer 52	**potato** 53	**overhead** 59

17 education	**23** impassable	**31** definition
32 information	**36** cemetery	**39** February
44 everyone	**47** interesting	**48** decorative
49 dictionary	**51** impossible	**54** January
55 analysis	**56** uninhabit	**60** illustration

Teacher Created Resources

Teacher Created Resources

Teacher Created Resources

Teacher Created Resources

Teacher Created Resources

Teacher Created Resources

Teacher Created Resources

Teacher Created Resources

Teacher Created Resources

Teacher Created Resources

Teacher Created Resources

Teacher Created Resources

Teacher Created Resources

Teacher Created Resources

Teacher Created Resources

Teacher Created Resources

Teacher Created Resources

Teacher Created Resources

Teacher Created Resources

Teacher Created Resources

Teacher Created Resources

Teacher Created Resources

Teacher Created Resources

Teacher Created Resources

Teacher Created Resources

Teacher Created Resources

Teacher Created Resources

Teacher Created Resources

Teacher Created Resources

Teacher Created Resources

Teacher Created Resources

Teacher Created Resources

Teacher Created Resources

Teacher Created Resources

Teacher Created Resources

Teacher Created Resources

Back to the Past

Skill: past tense verbs

Standard: uses grammatical and mechanical conventions in written compositions

Benchmark: uses verbs in written compositions (e.g., uses a wide variety of action verbs, past and present verb tenses, simple tenses, forms of regular verbs)

Materials

- Back to the Past game board
- Back to the Past cards
- Back to the Past answer key
- game markers (chips, tokens, etc.)

Suggested Use

- cooperative groups
- centers
- home connection
- tutorial

Directions (2 to 4 players)

1. Place the Back to the Past game board between players.

2. Lay Back to the Past cards face down for the draw pile.

3. Player A selects a card and spells the past form of the word. (Examples: bat = batted, eat = ate). Player B uses the answer key to check the answer. If the correct answer is given, Player A moves to the correct past time ending of the verb on the Back to the Past game board. For example, if *carry* is chosen, the player advances to *ied* because the past tense is *carried*. If the incorrect answer is given, Player A stays on the same place on the game board.

6. Play continues with Player B.

7. Play continues until a player goes completely around the board either landing on or going past START.

Variation

- Players go around the board a predetermined number of times.

Reminder

Past tense verbs tell about action in the past.
Examples: *jumped, hopped, ran, carried*

Back to the Past: Answer Key

bat	batted	double consonant, add *ed*
carry	carried	*y* to *i*, add *ed*
chop	chopped	double consonant, add *ed*
clean	cleaned	add *ed*
color	colored	add *ed*
comb	combed	add *ed*
correct	corrected	add *ed*
drink	drank	irregular
drive	drove	irregular
eat	ate	irregular
gather	gathered	add *ed*
go	went	irregular
greet	greeted	add *ed*
harvest	harvested	add *ed*
hop	hopped	double consonant, add *ed*
hope	hoped	take away *e*, add *ed*
jump	jumped	add *ed*
like	liked	take away *e*, add *ed*
marry	married	*y* to *i*, add *ed*
move	moved	add *ed*
order	ordered	add *ed*
play	played	add *ed*
ride	rode	irregular
run	ran	irregular
sit	sat	irregular
skip	skipped	double consonant, add *ed*
swim	swam, swum	irregular
tag	tagged	double consonant, add *ed*
tap	tapped	double consonant, add *ed*
type	typed	take away *e*, add *ed*
write	wrote	irregular

BACK TO THE PAST

START

Teacher Created Resources

Teacher Created Resources

Teacher Created Resources

Teacher Created Resources

Teacher Created Resources

Teacher Created Resources

Teacher Created Resources

Teacher Created Resources

Teacher Created Resources

Teacher Created Resources

Teacher Created Resources

Teacher Created Resources

Teacher Created Resources

Teacher Created Resources

Teacher Created Resources

Teacher Created Resources

Teacher Created Resources

Teacher Created Resources

Teacher Created Resources

Teacher Created Resources

Teacher Created Resources

Teacher Created Resources

Teacher Created Resources

Teacher Created Resources

Teacher Created Resources

Teacher Created Resources

Teacher Created Resources

Teacher Created Resources

Teacher Created Resources

Teacher Created Resources

Teacher Created Resources

Teacher Created Resources

Teacher Created Resources

Teacher Created Resources

Teacher Created Resources

Teacher Created Resources

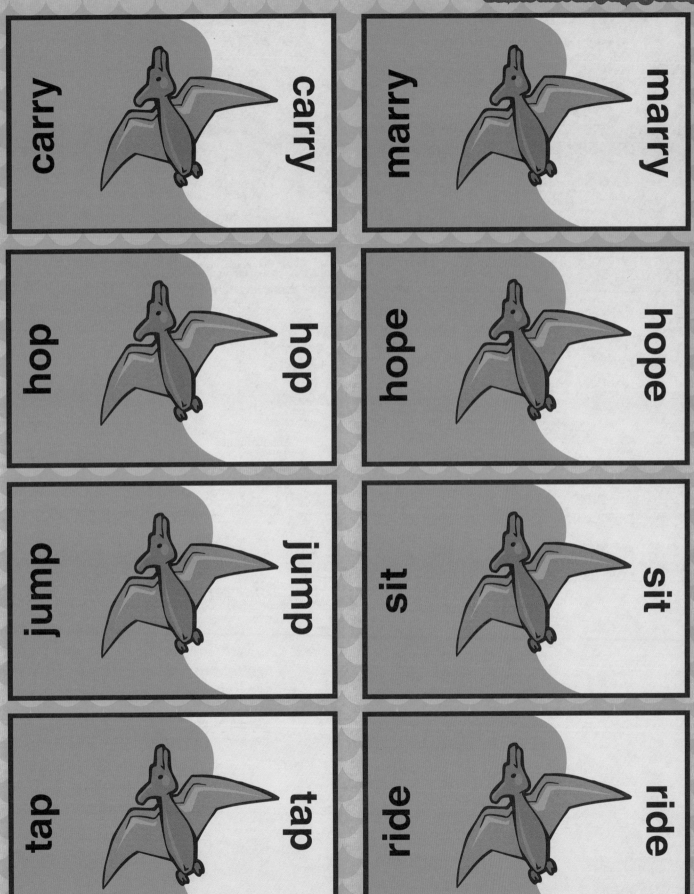

Teacher Created Resources

Teacher Created Resources

Teacher Created Resources

Teacher Created Resources

Teacher Created Resources

Teacher Created Resources

Teacher Created Resources

Teacher Created Resources

Teacher Created Resources

Teacher Created Resources

Teacher Created Resources

Teacher Created Resources

Teacher Created Resources

Teacher Created Resources

Teacher Created Resources

Teacher Created Resources

Teacher Created Resources

Teacher Created Resources

Teacher Created Resources

Teacher Created Resources

Teacher Created Resources

Teacher Created Resources

Teacher Created Resources

Teacher Created Resources

Teacher Created Resources

Teacher Created Resources

Teacher Created Resources

Teacher Created Resources

Teacher Created Resources

Teacher Created Resources

Teacher Created Resources

Teacher Created Resources

Teacher Created Resources

Teacher Created Resources

Teacher Created Resources

Teacher Created Resources

Teacher Created Resources

Teacher Created Resources

Teacher Created Resources

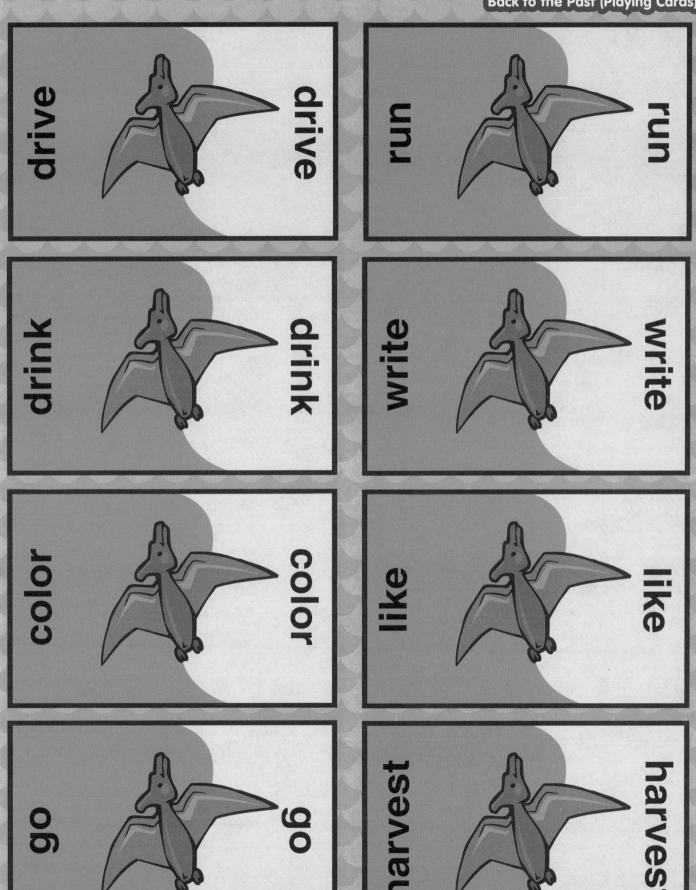

drive drive

run run

drink drink

write write

color color

like like

go go

harvest harvest

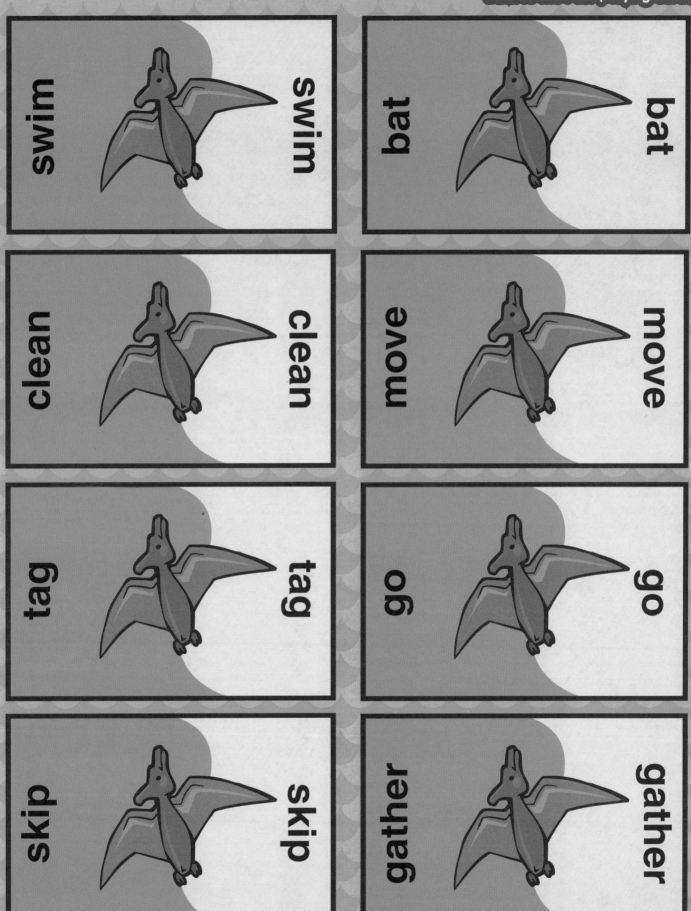

swim swim

bat bat

clean clean

move move

tag tag

go go

skip skip

gather gather

©Teacher Created Resources, Inc.

#8717 Standards-Based Activities & Games

Teacher Created Resources

Teacher Created Resources

Teacher Created Resources

Teacher Created Resources

Teacher Created Resources

Teacher Created Resources

Teacher Created Resources

Teacher Created Resources

Teacher Created Resources

Teacher Created Resources

Teacher Created Resources

Teacher Created Resources

Teacher Created Resources

Teacher Created Resources

Teacher Created Resources

Teacher Created Resources

Teacher Created Resources

Teacher Created Resources

Teacher Created Resources

Teacher Created Resources

Teacher Created Resources

Teacher Created Resources

Teacher Created Resources

Teacher Created Resources

Teacher Created Resources

Teacher Created Resources

Teacher Created Resources

Teacher Created Resources

Teacher Created Resources

Teacher Created Resources

Teacher Created Resources

Teacher Created Resources

Teacher Created Resources

Teacher Created Resources

Teacher Created Resources

Teacher Created Resources

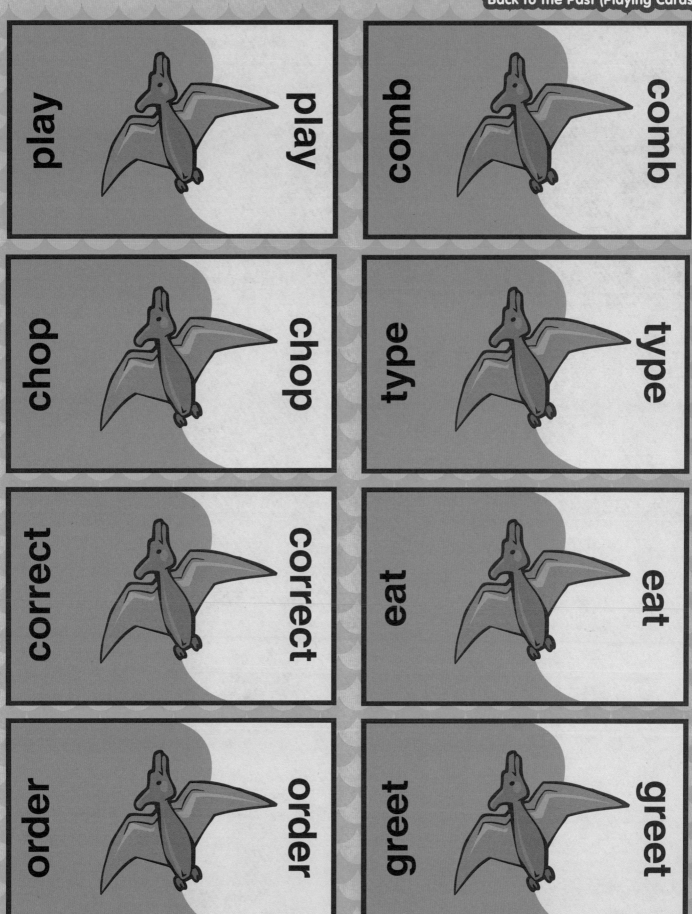

play play

comb comb

chop chop

type type

correct correct

eat eat

order order

greet greet

165

Skip Turn

Skip Turn

Skip Turn

Skip Turn

Go Back to Start

Go Back to Start

Go Back to Start

Go Back to Start

tag

tag

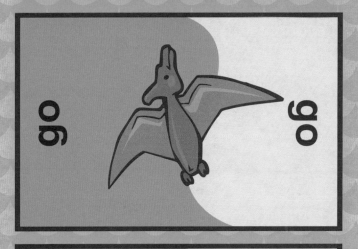

go

go

skip

skip

gather

gather

Teacher Created Resources	Teacher Created Resources	Teacher Created Resources	Teacher Created Resources
	Teacher Created Resources	Teacher Created Resources	Teacher Created Resources
Teacher Created Resources	Teacher Created Resources	Teacher Created Resources	Teacher Created Resources
	Teacher Created Resources	Teacher Created Resources	Teacher Created Resources
Teacher Created Resources	Teacher Created Resources	Teacher Created Resources	Teacher Created Resources
	Teacher Created Resources	Teacher Created Resources	Teacher Created Resources
Teacher Created Resources	Teacher Created Resources	Teacher Created Resources	Teacher Created Resources
	Teacher Created Resources	Teacher Created Resources	Teacher Created Resources
Teacher Created Resources	Teacher Created Resources	Teacher Created Resources	Teacher Created Resources

All in the Word Family

Skill: complex word families (*–ight, –ought, –aught*)

Standard: uses the general skills and strategies of the reading process

Benchmark: uses phonetic and structural analysis techniques, syntactic structure, and semantic context to decode words (e.g., complex word families)

Materials

- a copy of All in the Word Family game board for each player
- All in the Word Family game cards
- All in the Word Family answer key
- game markers (buttons, chips, etc.)

Suggested Use

- cooperative groups
- centers
- home connection
- tutorial

Directions (2 players)

1. Each player receives an All in the Word Family game board.
2. Place All in the Word Family cards as a draw pile between the two players.
3. Player A chooses and reads the top card of the draw pile, and completes the missing word in the sentence by selecting the correct word family (*–ight, –ought,* or *–aught*). Player B checks for the correct answer on the answer key. If correct, Player A places a game marker on the window that matches the correct word. If an incorrect answer is given or the space is already covered, the turn goes to the next player. The card is then placed at the bottom of the draw pile.
4. Play continues until one player's All in the Word Family game board is completely covered.

Variations

- Instead of covering all the windows, play continues until a player has covered three in a row.
- Players play on one game board until one player has covered three in a row.

Reminder

A <u>word family</u> is a group of words that are closely related to each other to form a "family."
Example: *bought, fought, sought*

All in the Word Family: Answer Key

1. light
2. thought
3. caught
4. bought
5. fright
6. fought
7. daughter
8. might
9. caught
10. bright
11. taught
12. brought
13. sought
14. flight
15. daughter

16. right
17. thought
18. caught
19. night
20. sight
21. taught
22. thought
23. daughter
24. fight
25. bought
26. caught
27. brought
28. might
29. taught
30. sought

Teacher Created Resources

Teacher Created Resources

Teacher Created Resources

Teacher Created Resources

Teacher Created Resources

Teacher Created Resources

Teacher Created Resources

Teacher Created Resources

Teacher Created Resources

Teacher Created Resources

Teacher Created Resources

Teacher Created Resources

Teacher Created Resources

Teacher Created Resources

Teacher Created Resources

Teacher Created Resources

Teacher Created Resources

Teacher Created Resources

Teacher Created Resources

Teacher Created Resources

Teacher Created Resources

Teacher Created Resources

Teacher Created Resources

Teacher Created Resources

Teacher Created Resources

Teacher Created Resources

Teacher Created Resources

Teacher Created Resources

Teacher Created Resources

Teacher Created Resources

Teacher Created Resources

Teacher Created Resources

Teacher Created Resources

The l_____ in the room is too bright.

1

I th_____ it was going to rain this morning.

2

The girls c_____ three large fish in the river.

3

My parents b_____ a new couch for the den.

4

The loud noise gave me a fr_____ .

5

My grandfather f_____ in the war.

6

My d_____er lost her gold ring at the park.

7

Adam m_____ go to school if he feels better.

8

Jenny c_____ a cold when she visited her cousins.

9

Maggie did not like the br_____ light.

10

Jill t_____ her little brother how to tie his shoes.

11

Ava br_____ her friend to the party.

12

The parents s_____ to raise money for books.

13

The fl_____ to Chicago was two hours late.

14

The young d_____er made a gift for her dad.

15

Teacher Created Resources

Teacher Created Resources

Teacher Created Resources

Teacher Created Resources

Teacher Created Resources

Teacher Created Resources

Teacher Created Resources

Teacher Created Resources

Teacher Created Resources

Teacher Created Resources

Teacher Created Resources

Teacher Created Resources

Teacher Created Resources

Teacher Created Resources

Teacher Created Resources

Teacher Created Resources

Teacher Created Resources

Teacher Created Resources

Teacher Created Resources

Teacher Created Resources

Teacher Created Resources

Teacher Created Resources

Teacher Created Resources

Teacher Created Resources

Teacher Created Resources

Teacher Created Resources

Teacher Created Resources

Teacher Created Resources

Teacher Created Resources

Teacher Created Resources

Teacher Created Resources

Teacher Created Resources

Teacher Created Resources

Teacher Created Resources

Teacher Created Resources

Jordan throws with his r_____ hand.

16

I th_____ it was going to rain this morning.

17

The spider c_____ two flies in the web.

18

At n_____ the desert animals hunt for food.

19

The fireworks at night are an awesome s_____ .

20

The clerk t_____ me how to count change.

21

I th_____ the game started at 7:00.

22

My youngest d_____er was in the school play.

23

What was the f_____ on the playground about?

24

My mom b_____ green and blue paint for my room.

25

I c_____ the ball before it went over the fence.

26

Ryan br_____ his dog to the vet for a check-up.

27

The football team m_____ win the game.

28

Who t_____ you how to play the piano?

29

My brother s_____ to find his missing bike.

30

Teacher Created Resources

Teacher Created Resources

Teacher Created Resources

Teacher Created Resources

Teacher Created Resources

Teacher Created Resources

Teacher Created Resources

Teacher Created Resources

Teacher Created Resources

Teacher Created Resources

Teacher Created Resources

Teacher Created Resources

Teacher Created Resources

Teacher Created Resources

Teacher Created Resources

Teacher Created Resources

Teacher Created Resources

Teacher Created Resources

Teacher Created Resources

Teacher Created Resources

Teacher Created Resources

Teacher Created Resources

Teacher Created Resources

Teacher Created Resources

Teacher Created Resources

Teacher Created Resources

Teacher Created Resources

Teacher Created Resources

Teacher Created Resources

Teacher Created Resources

Teacher Created Resources

Teacher Created Resources

Teacher Created Resources

Teacher Created Resources

Teacher Created Resources

Teacher Created Resources